Breaking the Grass Ceiling

Breaking the Grass Ceiling
Women, Weed & Business

Breaking the Grass Ceiling has a registered trademark application pending.

FIRST EDITION

FIRST PRINTING FEBRUARY 2017

COVER DESIGN
Emily Burchell

EDITOR
Emma Ritchie

WWW.GRASSCEILINGBOOK.COM

ISBN: 1541096592
ISBN 13: 9781541096592

Breaking the Grass Ceiling

Women, Weed & Business

Ashley Picillo & Lauren Devine

To Mary Jane—*the female that brought each of us here*

Table of Contents

Breaking the Grass Ceiling

Ashley Picillo
Lauren Devine

Preface

I DIDN'T SMOKE pot growing up—*ever*—not once. I was raised to believe it was an addictive and harmful drug used by lazy people who weren't going to amount to anything. For this reason, many of my friends, family members, and former co-workers were surprised to see me make a professional transition into the cannabis industry. This journey into cannabis began in early 2014. I flew out to Colorado from NYC thinking my work in cannabis was temporary. Back home, I had the safety net of a full-time job offer waiting for me; however, by the time I was slated to start work, my temporary visit had turned into a life-changing relocation. I didn't jump into the industry with much risk; I had no kids at home to be concerned about and I was joining the movement after much of its initial stigma had faded. I was able to dive in knowing that, if I later regretted my decision, I could quickly and quietly make my exit and return to a full-time job and furnished apartment in NYC. My gratitude for the luxury of that situation is what drove me to write this book. I felt compelled to shine a spotlight on and pay homage to the many women who pioneered this industry *for me* and others like me.

I want to draw focus to the activist and mother who moved to Colorado so her son's life could be saved by cannabis oil as he battled Dravet syndrome; to the doctor who chose to stand up to the DEA to ensure that cannabis efficacy research has a place in our future; to the dispensary owner who tackled cannabis as a social justice issue in defense of her brother who was imprisoned for a non-violent marijuana crime. *These* are the women who paved the way for other women wanting to enter this industry, and this book aims to share their awe-inspiring stories as well as the lessons they've learned.

As this book came together, I realized something I inherently knew but had not spent a lot of time considering: our movement is equal parts activism and business and neither part is more important than the other. I came into this industry for one core reason: I saw a huge professional opportunity for *myself*. At the time, I was a 26-year-old female who was driven, hungry, and bored by the career prospects I saw before me. I wanted to create something, and knew that building my own company from the ground up within a developing industry was a rare opportunity. I remember reading in school, decades ago, about the invention of the automobile and how it fundamentally changed American culture by giving way to travel, exploration, fast food restaurants, highways, and hotels. I remember the first time I surfed the web, sent messages to my middle school friends on AOL Instant Messenger, and did my first school paper with research I had found online rather than in the school library. Monumental, culture-shifting opportunities like these do not present themselves frequently, and while I wasn't sure exactly how I would carve out my niche in cannabis, I knew I wanted to get involved. I recognized that this was my chance to be creative, exercise my independence, prove my resourcefulness, and positively influence an industry in need of fresh ideas and energy. I got into this industry *solely* because I saw it as an attractive entrepreneurial opportunity for myself—*until I moved to Denver.*

I can tell you now that what I grew up learning as a child was bullshit. Marijuana isn't a drug, and you won't hear me call it that anymore. It is a plant—a highly medicinal one—that is widely consumed by an enormously diverse group of people. I am willing to bet that most people picking up this book either are or know someone who is benefiting from cannabis, whether it's their next door neighbor, a colleague from work, or a friend suffering from a medical condition. My point is this: I didn't come into this industry as an activist, *but I became one.*

This plant is powerful in so many ways. Beyond its medicinal benefits, this plant can teach us—even people like me, who grew up in staunch opposition to cannabis—so much. It has taught me to be more open minded and less quick to cast judgment on others. It has taught me to ask more questions, specifically as it relates to claims about marijuana in the area of healthcare. It has the power to change minds by way of demonstration and it shows us collectively, everyday, what it can do. I am inspired by the business owners, members of the activist community, and the many people who identify as both. All of the many people who wake up in the morning to fight for legal access to cannabis because it's absolutely, unequivocally right keep me going. I don't believe you can have capitalism without activism and I don't believe I could be one without the other. This plant fundamentally changed me for the better.

I have been asked what the title of this book means many times, and my answer has changed substantially from when we began our interviews; to the halfway point of our writing process; to now, as I write this preface to complete these final pages. A glass ceiling is the barrier many women struggle to surpass in business. Beyond the glass await equal salaries, executive level roles and responsibilities, and many other opportunities that have been historically reserved for men. A *Grass Ceiling* is the same concept, but as it pertains to cannabis. Even though the marijuana business has been promoted as a more welcoming environment for women compared to other male-dominated industries, women still have to fight to earn and maintain equality in the workplace. Several women who started companies in the early days have grappled to hold onto the very things they built. Some women have lost their companies all together. Women need to help one another, but that will not be enough. Breaking through the ceiling requires a fundamental change in thinking, by women, by other minorities, and—most especially—by men.

Over the past three years, I have experienced a lot: I've had both women *and* men take me under their wings and I've had both women *and* men try to hold me back from achieving my goals. It is my firm belief that women, specifically, have an obligation to encourage and support one another. While speaking with Jaime Lewis of Mountain Medicine, she shared that her goal when hiring women is to "hire, train, and mentor women who will rise up and compete with [her] directly." In order to reach our full potential as a gender, that's exactly the way it should be. These women are not sharing their stories to bash men or to point fingers at specific people or companies with whom they have had poor experiences. They are sharing their stories to inspire and educate so that we may continue moving forward *together*. *Together* we have the unique opportunity to create an industry with no ceiling at all.

Breaking the Grass Ceiling is a collection of stories shared by women who have carved out opportunities for themselves and for others in the cannabis industry. They have done this by helping other women to gain access to medicine; by helping women find their callings and careers; by having difficult conversations over a decade ago, at a time when speaking in favor of cannabis was incredibly risky. And even though the work is far from done, it is because of these pioneering efforts that many more women will be able to successfully follow suit and continue down this path beyond the glass.

I am humbled by and grateful to the 21 women Lauren and I had the pleasure of speaking with for this book: Betty Aldworth, Giadha Aguirre de Carcer, Jessica Billingsley, Amy Dawn Bourlon-Hilterbran, Diane Czarkowski, Amy Dilullo, Julie Dooley, Diane Fornbacher, Rachel K. Gillette, Karson Humiston, Wanda James, Kristi Kelly, Heidi Keyes, Karin Lazarus, Jaime Lewis, Maureen McNamara, Genifer Murray, Amy Poinsett, Meg Sanders, Dr. Sue Sisley and Susan Squibb. I also want to acknowledge one of my biggest supporters, Alex Witkowicz, a man who reminds me everyday that he believes in me and that there are so many men who want to be our allies. And last, but absolutely not least, Lauren – who answered my phone call on an average Tuesday in mid-December 2016 and enthusiastically told me this project was possible and necessary. This would not have come together without Lauren.

During my time in cannabis, I have worked with some of the best leaders and companies and have found myself an exceptional group of friends. I have also enjoyed visiting and working in a number of different cultivation facilities throughout Colorado. Over the years I have I've been asked a few times what my favorite part of the industry is. Beyond the wonderful people I have met, I've come to realize that simply being around these special plants is a privilege, one I do not take for granted. I especially treasure the times I've spent in my favorite cultivation room, the one where the mother plants are tended. And there is significance to that title: ***this entire story begins with the female.***

—*Ashley Picillo*

Kristi Lee Kelly

CANNABIS ENTREPRENEUR

"Everything this plant touches creates an opportunity for innovation."

KRISTI LEE KELLY, an intelligent and empathetic businesswoman who likes to be referred to as a "cannabis entrepreneur," has a career with many diverse facets. She is a strategic and passionate serial enterpriser and advocate, and was driven to the cannabis industry by her empathy for others. Her tone genuine and warm, she describes a feeling of connectedness and believes collective positivity can be a powerful impetus for great change within both the cannabis space and the world. Kristi currently serves as the Executive Director of the Marijuana Industry Group (MIG), described on MIG's website as "Colorado's first and largest trade association for licensed marijuana businesses." Prior to her current position, she was an owner and operator of a group of high-quality medical marijuana cultivation facilities, a marijuana-infused product manufacturer, and dispensaries in the greater Denver area. Throughout her career, she has helped start numerous industry organizations, nonprofits, and businesses committed to education, safe access, and responsible business operations. Kristi is also a founding board member of the Fourth Corner Credit Union—described on Fourth Corner's website as "the cannabis industry's first financial institution." The firstborn of her generation to a very large "founding family" of Washington, DC's Chinatown—"the trifecta of community, family, and education were established as core values" early in Kristi's life. Those core values are apparent in her work and in her general outlook on the future of the cannabis industry.

As an account management executive for several advertising and marketing firms in the DC area, Kristi spent many years serving as the liaison between her agency and her clients. She was involved in business development and research for companies operating in luxury retail, real estate, pharmaceuticals, and government, to name only a few. Having "come of age in the dot-com era," Kristi had seen many of her friends and colleagues achieve great success within the tech industry and "never thought [she] would see such astronomical growth in [her] lifetime." It was at her wedding in 2009 that Kristi first considered getting into cannabis. Because tech was never really of interest to her, she recalls thinking: "If there is ever another opportunity like [the dot-com boom], I want in. Some of our wedding guests were talking about how happy, or not happy, they were with their current jobs, and the topic of cannabis came up. I said, 'If you ever start something, let me know.'"

At that time, Kristi and her husband thought they might simply invest in friends' companies, hoping to earn some residual income to fund her work with various international charity organizations. However, in 2009, Kristi became an investor in medical cannabis, and in 2010, moved out to Colorado to dedicate herself to the advancement of patient access to medical marijuana. Her husband, Nathan, joined her a few months later for the same purpose.

Kristi is grateful that her family and friends have been "eternally supportive of everything that [she's] done," including her decision to enter cannabis. However, she admits that, "with immediate family members who work for the federal government, and in particular the US Attorney's Office, there was obviously some trepidation." Nathan and Kristi were entering unfamiliar territory, but were enthusiastic to navigate this new path together and confident they could always return to their network of family and friends back home for guidance and support.

> I was giving up a career with a clear succession plan in exchange for uncertainty and potential future unemployability, or worse. My husband was my rock, but also my biggest challenger. We were newlyweds, and we opted for a crazy beginning to our life together. Our family and friends stood by when we weren't sure how we were going to pay the bills, and they rejoiced with us when things finally turned the corner. I was initially hurt that there were some members of my family who didn't feel comfortable visiting me in Colorado, but we are past all of that now.

Kristi misses the family she does not see often, but strives to keep in touch: "Our interactions require discipline to stay connected."

The advertising and marketing world that Kristi came from was surprisingly—and wonderfully—not as male dominated or hostile compared to some of the circumstances and experiences other women have faced.

When Kristi worked in DC, she had a female mentor and felt the corporate culture was very supportive of females and their collective success in the workplace. Many of her colleagues were women and she felt very comfortable in that "collaborative and encouraging environment." As she transitioned into cannabis, however, she did not find this to be the case. "It was a shock to come into the cannabis space. It was male dominated when I began my career here. It took me a while to find a place that felt comfortable where I could develop the relationships that I have today." When it comes to seeing more women break through the cannabis industry's grass ceiling and take on leadership roles, Kristi suggests: "It *became* the norm—it didn't *start* as the norm." She goes on to describe a troubling time when she observed the disparity in cannabis negatively affecting her female peers:

> It was hard for me to see strong women become vulnerable. Not being on the inside, I can't ever fully know what happened when they embarked on their cannabis journey, or why things transpired the way that they did . . . but it was hard to see that happen to people who had worked so tirelessly to advance the industry as a whole. This is an industry where you absolutely cannot leave the details at the door.

The same "details" Kristi refers to—the crucial nature of obtaining proper representation and documentation to ensure every entrepreneur protects herself and her business—are so vital that they are also emphasized by almost every other woman in the cannabis industry. Still, always looking for the silver lining, Kristi reassures, "Those experiences have only created stronger and better people and produced better opportunities." The cannabis industry almost perfectly exemplifies the familiar expression "when one door closes, another one opens"; As a constantly adapting and pivoting entrepreneur, Kristi deliberately approaches times of struggle from the perspective that every problem has the power to yield potential opportunity.

In this industry, I feel that it's more like, another 25 doors open. It's an explosion of opportunity because we've created something that others perceive to have value. We are a part of the world's first regulated cannabis economy. The lessons learned from the ground up are invaluable. With the knowledge that we have, we could potentially save millions of dollars of investors' money in mistakes and convert it to profit. Those entities that are fortunate enough to engage these women who have been here since the beginning can only add to their exponential growth, relative to engaging another who does not have that knowledge.

Kristi is an open book when it comes to sharing the keys to her success and offering advice to the next generation of women in cannabis. She wants all women to feel empowered to come into this space. She pauses to collect her thoughts for a moment, then offers: "Find a mentor. Have a lawyer you love document everything. Trust your instincts." This is sound advice for anyone hoping to carve out a permanent place in a rapidly expanding field. Kristi's "marijuana mentor," Nicholas 'Nick' King, is the first person she met in the cannabis industry, just as the rulemaking process was starting to be articulated. Nick is the founder and former owner of Alpine Herbal Wellness Center. Kristi says it was "amazing" learning from and working alongside Nick.

A group of us co-founded ACT4CO [Association of Cannabis Trades for Colorado]. We worked together as a board. That organization provided the foundation of my regulatory understanding, which I think is the most important thing for a cannabis owner or cannabis operator to have. Nick was an educator; he took an inclusive approach which resulted in hundreds of businesses learning and having access to information they might not have had access to otherwise. The businesses were all competitors, but he created an environment where competitors could be colleagues and friends who helped each other out. If we can do well while the world is watching, then we will be doing a service to the cannabis industry as a whole.

Nick serving as a mentor to Kristi is a clear example of how important men are in the quest for gender equality in the business world. The supportive and collaborative environment he was able to create, where competitors are able to work together, will—undoubtedly—benefit the industry. And when an industry with so much opportunity and innovation thrives, there is favorable socioeconomic impact worldwide.

In addition to her business savvy and willingness to dive headfirst into this new industry, Kristi's "dedication to social responsibility and global social change, [her] outlook on life, and respect for the human experience is the most important contributor to [her] success in business." Kristi feels that the high point of her experience in the cannabis realm is "happening right now—at this point in time." She credits Meg Sanders, of MiNDFUL, for being the first to tell her that "a year in cannabis is like dog years," and explains that, in just a few years, many things have changed for the better. "I have had the privilege of being involved in cannabis since 2009. It's now at a place—the culmination of the good, the bad, the indifferent—where we are on the precipice, everything is at a critical inflection point and coming together right now. The opportunities for the future are so exciting."

One of the exciting opportunities on Kristi's horizon is her involvement with The Fourth Corner Credit Union, the first financial institution in the world to receive a charter to serve the marijuana community. At the time of publication, Kristi shared that she is the only licensed marijuana business representative on the board. This is a huge step forward for the cannabis industry, which has struggled with its desperate need for banking solutions. "Their work has inspired other financial institutions to fill a void in our community; however, the credit union awaits a federal court decision so they can open their doors." The day those doors open will mark a major turning point in how marijuana businesses operate in the financial realm.

Newcomers to the industry and veteran entrepreneurs alike recognize the potential and opportunity this industry promises. To Kristi, the most exciting possibilities lie in the field of medical advancements because so many people will be impacted. She admits:

> I have always been a bleeding heart, and the reason I put money into cannabis was not to *be in cannabis,* but to, hopefully, have access to resources that would allow me to go into developing countries and help people. I stayed in cannabis because I realized that I didn't need to go halfway around the world to be helpful; cannabis is doing that right here. The [cannabis] industry is about to take a massive leap forward.

Another of Kristi's personal highlights is her contribution to the CannAbility Foundation, a patient advocacy and resource network for families of children living with conditions and disabilities that can be helped by cannabis, of which she is a founding trustee. The CannAbility Foundation is led by Stacey Lynn, the mother of Jack Splitt. Jack was the inspiration for Jack's Law and Jack's Amendment, which allow sick children safe access to medical cannabis in school. According to their website, CannAbility's mission is to provide families of sick children with access to resources and medical cannabis so that "the families can worry less and spend more time focusing on their kids—which is really what's most important." Kristi continues:

> Jack sadly passed away this summer [2016], but not before he changed some of the most staunch, anti-cannabis Colorado legislators' positions to be supportive of cannabis policies, not before he inspired the National Council of Women Legislators to pass a resolution that any of them who had medical cannabis laws would simultaneously work for protection of sick kids who needed safe access. In that, Jack's legacy lives on.

I got into this industry so I could help people. Whatever you're trying to change: economic development, gender issues or social change—any social consciousness issues, really—you can do it *or* you can empower other people to do it. What Stacey has done with CannAbility is so amazing. I'm very proud of the minimal things I've done to help make that possible.

Kristi's spirituality contributes to her disarming humility, and she acknowledges that forces beyond herself and the support of others are imperative drivers of any significant change. It is not easy for her to take credit for her achievements and contributions. This is not because she is undeserving, but rather because Kristi prefers to give credit to others who have helped her to reach personal success.

Scientifically speaking, we are energy, and, therefore, we all exist on the same plane. Call it universal energy or call it whatever you want, the point is: we are all connected. In the past year, I have felt such a compelling pull from the sisterhood of women in cannabis, and I like that this book is amplifying that bond because it is so important. There is something so potent happening in our world right now that is magnetically attracting us to each other to offer resources, to help each other through good times and bad. There are super strong, super intelligent women orbiting around each other right now in cannabis. It's such a powerful force in my life, and I welcome it.

Kristi Lee Kelly's future looks limitless as she expands upon her plans for her work. "At Marijuana Industry Group, we will continue to focus on advancing the future of regulated cannabis. Policy, to me, is the armor that licensees *must* have in order to protect and expand the model that we have in place." She also directs her focus outward and mentions, "There are a lot of really exciting companies that are on the precipice of being known to the greater public and I cannot wait for them to matriculate." Kristi closes with a final message of enthusiastic optimism and gratitude:

The potential that this plant has in creating opportunities in every direction: technology, science, creative banking solutions, greenhouse innovations—everything this plant touches creates an opportunity for innovation. I cannot wait for the future because I feel like there are so many opportunities. It is my absolute honor to be a part of it.

Jaime Lewis

FOUNDER AND CEO OF MOUNTAIN MEDICINE

"I don't need the red carpet and I don't need anyone to open the door for me. But I do need you to get out of my fucking way if you're blocking me from getting through the door."

JAIME LEWIS DID not come into the cannabis industry to build an empire all alone. She's here to make sure her friends, closest allies, and peers build empires, too. Often described as a "total powerhouse," "badass," and the most "sincere of friends," Jaime is a woman whose guidance is sought out by industry newcomers and seasoned veterans alike because she is authentic, inspiring, and empowering with her "we can do it" attitude. Her experience in the male-dominated restaurant industry prepared her well for the world of cannabis. She isn't afraid to challenge the norm and she doesn't need any favors—she just needs those who doubt her to stay out of her way. Confident and resilient, she strives to always "do good by being good," a phrase she is known for repeating to her "herd," the employees who work alongside her each day. She is the "Mama Goat" of Mountain Medicine, an edibles company developing high quality products for patients and recreational users alike, and at the head of several other companies in states on the verge of massive growth. Jaime is a compassionate advocate and a competent businesswoman who consistently pulls other women up with her as she crashes through the grass ceiling.

Before Jaime's career in cannabis, she worked as a professional chef. Classically trained and hailing from Le Cordon Bleu Culinary Arts Program, she recalls her serious ambition "to become a James Beard culinary rockstar!" Following her passion for the culinary arts, Jaime moved to San Francisco and began cooking in highly acclaimed kitchens, including a Michelin-rated three star restaurant. Jaime was very successful in this world, but it took an enormous amount of work and some thick skin to achieve it.

> I busted my ass in a world dominated by men, and that's when I realized that I, too, can be quite dominant. [That world] gave me my work ethic. It gave me the concept of teamwork, and I learned about how to work as a team to get things done under the gun. However, none of this work was anywhere near as grueling as cannabis has been.

In 2006, while working as a chef in San Francisco, Jaime remained passionate about cannabis, a plant she had "always been a fan of, that was around [her] in some way, shape, or form for many years." Growing up in Northern California, cannabis was always a part of her environment and firmly established in the local culture; Jaime says her love of cannabis has been "lifelong." Her first foray into cannabis, outside her own personal use, came about when Jaime learned that the father of one of her closest friends was HIV positive. She remembers him being in serious pain and struggling to eat. He had been treating his symptoms with cannabis, but became so sick he could no longer smoke. Jaime began working on recipes for edibles in her kitchen at home, fusing together her culinary background, long time love of cannabis, and compassion for others.

Jaime's first trials in the kitchen were during a time where you couldn't simply go online and look up a recipe for this kind of product. She tinkered with various formulations, her drive for culinary perfection moving her to continue reformulating and experimenting in new ways. As she continued perfecting her recipes, Jaime met with other HIV patients who were also extremely sick, and created medical marijuana edibles for them as part of a compassionate co-op.

> I remember a specific conversation with a gentleman who was HIV positive and he shared how powerful the edibles had been in his ability to feel better. It was an intense and emotional conversation because I was speaking with someone who had been destroyed by HIV who was crediting these edibles with helping him to feel better and to regain his appetite. Being a fat kid myself who fucking loves food—edibles being an extension of that—and having a conversation with a man who literally had tears of joy on his face because he could, for the first time in a long time, enjoy his mother's recipe of spaghetti and meatballs—that was emotional. I've always been a compassionate person and an advocate, and cooking for people is part of that. Food is a true way to care for people. And that's when I decided to go all-in.

Going "all-in" wouldn't be easy in California, a state with a robust cannabis culture and history, but lacking regulations. Jaime's goal was not to continue making edibles in her kitchen on a small (and, at the time, illegal) scale. She wanted to do it the right way, and in a big way, so she set her sights on Colorado. This was a challenging decision for Jaime to make as she absolutely loves her home state of California and was reluctant to leave.

> Building a business in California would have been like building my business on sand—very difficult because there were no regulations. It was the right time for me to look at Colorado. It was right before Obama was elected and it was a volatile time in the industry. I had heard from friends in Colorado that the state was going to regulate the market, a concept that was extremely foreign to me coming from California, so I packed up and decided to make the transition to Colorado.

Upon her arrival to Colorado, Jaime wasted no time getting involved in the industry. She began paying close attention to the regulatory process, learning everything she could about the rules, and started the Cannabis Business Alliance where she was a very active member. In that same year, she founded Mountain Medicine, a marijuana infused product (MIP) manufacturer focused on developing the highest quality medical edibles and distributing them throughout the state of Colorado. Mountain Medicine introduced a recreational line in 2014. Jaime's culinary background served her well as she designed her entire commercial kitchen space and supervised its construction while also developing gourmet formulations and recipes. Jaime then joined forces with a team of cannabis entrepreneurs to build out a cultivation and dispensary business while simultaneously managing Mountain Medicine.

Beyond her work and success building and operating cannabis companies, Jaime remains extremely active in supporting the industry through her work on various advisory boards. Jaime is in her sixth year of serving on the board of the National Cannabis Industry Association in addition to her role as founder and former Chair of the Cannabis Business Alliance. She points out that, by being involved with these organizations, she is able to help change the conversation around safe and responsible cannabis use at both the state and national levels. Furthermore, a significant amount of Jaime's profits go toward supporting a range of organizations, including the Drug Policy Alliance (DPA), Students for Sensible Drug Policy (SSDP), the Chun Association, the Marijuana Policy Project (MPP), and One Colorado. While her journey has been mostly positive, Jaime has also experienced low points, as many people do when launching a new business, evaluating partnerships, and setting off to do something no one has ever done before.

In 2010, Jaime experienced two major blows to her progress: a falling out with business partners and the loss of her fiance. The company Jaime had formed with her partners "defined" her, and the day that she no longer had that company, she remembers feeling completely lost. "Losing my fiance, my company, and a role in the company that defined me was so, so hard. I didn't know what I was going to do the next day. I was down and I felt gutted." For most people, this level of loss may have been enough to make them pack their bags, and head home. But Jaime resolved to learn from the experience and to use her pain to fuel her next endeavor.

> I started by asking Jaime—*me* Jaime, not *the business owner* Jaime—what makes me happy and what do [I] want to do next? Through this process, I proved to myself how powerful, resilient, and smart I could be. The feeling of pulling myself out of a dark place and recreating myself was incredibly powerful. I promised myself to not let myself become a victim. Instead, I sought out people who could mentor and teach me, and began to rebuild.

Mountain Medicine, the company Jaime still owned, would now receive her full attention. She poured herself into building a business that she was proud of, both from a product and from a social responsibility perspective.

"I wanted to build a company that did good things in the community and was good to, and supportive of, others."

In 2016, in addition to running and scaling Mountain Medicine, Jaime began working in Massachusetts as she launched a cannabis business alongside her partners in the state—a process that did not come without its own unique challenges. Jaime describes going to neighborhood meetings set up by the state for communities to share their concerns with teams that were eager to discuss gaining approval and support for their marijuana businesses. "People were [verbally] attacking us, throwing out all kinds of *Reefer Madness* propaganda bullshit. It was tough, especially because, while we still deal with some of this in Colorado, it's much more normalized now. This was like starting over."

Massachusetts, which only legalized medical marijuana in 2012 and recreational marijuana in 2016, is four years behind Colorado; this contextualizes the concerns expressed by Massachusetts residents as there was similar pushback in Colorado at the time of Amendment 64's passing. Instead of steering away from these attacks, Jaime had an epiphany: "It hit me while I was there listening to all of these people sharing their fears and concerns—this is exactly where I need to be. I don't need to be in California or Colorado, I need to be here advocating for and educating the people of Massachusetts."

Although part of Jaime has always wanted to return to California, she has embraced that her efforts are needed in other markets, arguably far more than they are in her home state where cannabis culture has been accepted for so long.

I have done a lot of reputable work over the years as it relates to advocacy and education, work that has the power to change minds and to start new dialogues. I also enjoy proving people wrong and want to be here [in Massachusetts] where there is a lot of work to do in changing minds and stereotypes and educating people who are currently very fearful and thinking about marijuana in the same way that they think about heroin. It's been frustrating, but I will continue pushing through so people stop seeing cannabis as a detriment to their communities.

She is relentless in her pursuits, but humble and realistic as she considers *how* she will accomplish this, citing a number of women who she has and will continue to lean on.

> Karson [Humiston] and Susannah [Grossman] both remind me a lot of who I was when I was younger. They are both full of fire. Susannah will likely be one of my toughest competitors if she ever goes off on her own to launch her own company, and that's what I want in my staff. I seek out women who have that potential [to compete with me], and I support them however I can in their pursuits.

Jaime is not afraid of competition, nor is she a woman who ever feels threatened by other powerful women. She has the track record to prove this, actively looking for the most talented and powerful women to join her in her efforts. "To do everything I want to do, I need a strong team. I seek women out because every role I need to fill requires so much multitasking and women are amazing multitaskers. I truly believe women are stronger because we have had to go through so much in history to get this strength." Jaime cites countless examples of when women have excelled, dating back to the time of hunters and gatherers. She also adds that, in addition to her strength, she is fiercely independent: "I don't need to be acknowledged for being a 'powerhouse' woman. I don't need the red carpet and I don't need anyone to open the door for me. But I do need you to get out of my fucking way if you're blocking me from getting through the door."

She is outstandingly ambitious and will not settle for anything less than an empire, one run by powerful women and designed to serve the medical marijuana community in an impactful way. As she reflects on her journey thus far, Jaime is proud that her efforts were built upon a genuine commitment to patients and a never waning core of compassion. She has enormous plans for herself, her team, and the industry in general, encouraging more women to join her in mentoring new talent without feeling fearful or threatened.

> When women don't support one another, we cut ourselves off at the knees. When women don't genuinely support other women, and, instead, suppress talent out of fear of competition, it's almost worse than if a man were to do that. Encouraging and mentoring others is part of being a leader. We can create such a powerhouse [industry] if we continue supporting one another. Personally, I don't find myself feeling jealous or controlling of other women; I'm not afraid of hiring a woman smarter than myself.

Jaime has mentored, advised, supported, and inspired many women in the industry, some of whom offer her kudos in this book.

> For me, it was about the fight and the true love to force people to change the conversation about cannabis. I love people, food, and cannabis—I found now I'm good at putting teams together and building big companies too. I have a good track record of doing well at this because I sincerely love it. I often tell women this: you will only be as successful as you can be if you're doing something you love. So whatever the fuck you choose to do, love what you do. It's the only way you'll truly be successful.

Through her career in cannabis, Jaime Lewis wants to prove that women *are* strong leaders and *will* be the "brave, intelligent, sensitive" people who continue to shift the paradigms of power and gender in our society. As far as Jaime's personal goals and plans for her business, she declares:

> I want to build an empire. That's what I want. I want to build an amazing company that goes national. I want to create one of the

best companies to work for. I want to give back to those who have pushed this movement forward while developing some kickass products. I'm here to build a fucking empire. How that ends up, I have no idea. And I'm good with that.

———

Diane Czarkowski

FOUNDING PARTNER AT CANNA ADVISORS

"I had so many barriers to fight through, but it made me determined to do better than them as a way of saying fuck you."

DIANE CZARKOWSKI ISN'T new to working in a male dominated industry; she spent over a decade as an outside sales woman for various high tech companies during the dot-com era. At first glance, she appears almost demure, but make no mistake, she can spit fire. A seasoned veteran of business, real estate, and high tech, Diane excelled in multiple highly competitive industries before she joined the cannabis industry. With her husband, Jay Czarkowski, she is a Founding Partner at Canna Advisors, one of the top consulting firms in the industry supporting clients from coast to coast.

Di worked for several large firms during her years in technology, making many important contacts and building strong relationships. Most notably, Di met her now husband, Jay, who was also climbing the ranks of the tech industry and finding success. She remarks, "I was there during a time that mirrors the cannabis industry right now—when high tech was experiencing explosive growth." It was quite common for professionals in the early days of high tech to bounce from one company to the next, and Diane did just that, accelerating her career through a largely male dominated environment. In 2002, when the tech company for which Di was working announced that all of its employees would be required to relocate to Texas, she decided it was time to make a significant professional change. "At the time, Jay had already left high tech himself. He got his Commercial General Contractor's license and he wanted to pursue real estate development in Colorado. I decided I would get my real estate license and, together, we started our first company." The duo went on to spend several years splitting time between Steamboat Springs, Colorado, and the Denver and Boulder areas, developing homes on a large scale. Business was booming. Diane and Jay got married and bought a home, and life seemed to be good—until 2008 when the real estate market began to collapse. "I remember vividly sitting down with Jay and asking ourselves, 'What's next?'"

As the real estate market diminished, the Czarkowskis began downsizing their development company and looked into subleasing the office space they had just off the popular Pearl Street Mall in downtown Boulder.

Before long, they were approached by two different groups interested in converting the Czarkowski's location into a marijuana dispensary. Di recalls her disbelief: "Initially I thought these groups were nuts!" She had never *really* been a cannabis user and had a limited understanding about the plant and its medicinal benefits. "I was not big into the culture. I was in my mid-to-late twenties the first time I tried it. I had never bought it, only trying it when others had it out." But the proposal stirred up a different idea for Jay: "I remember Jay trying to convince me to open the dispensary ourselves and I was not interested at all. One day he looked at me and said, 'We are either going to have a really long, hard road in real estate, or we can take $15 to $20k, turn this place into a dispensary, and try the road into the pot business!'" Diane weighed her options and realized Jay was right. Using the experience and wisdom they had gained from their time spent in tech and real estate, Diane felt confident that they could navigate the challenges of an emerging and expanding industry with the enormous potential to thrive. So they decided to dive in.

As one of the only Colorado women working in cannabis at that time, Di often reflects on her initial reluctance and how much she fretted, fearing the unknown. "I needed to know that we were not going to be put in prison, leaving our children orphaned! . . . We spent a lot of time speaking with attorneys before taking the leap. I needed to hear from others who were watching the industry closely that this was going to be okay for us." Diane received the confirmation she needed from various attorneys shortly thereafter and their work began. On Friday, October 13, 2009, before Colorado's regulations had been released, Di and Jay opened the doors to their new business Boulder Kind Care (BKC). In 2011, when licenses were formally issued, BKC earned one of the first state and local licenses in Colorado.

After several years operating their dispensary and associated cultivation facility, Jay and Di sold BKC and "had no idea" what they would do next. In late 2012, the Czarkowskis received a call from a group in Connecticut seeking their expertise in application writing—this marked the creation of Canna Advisors. "We won one of only four cultivation licenses in the state of Connecticut, so we knew we could do it." Armed with their collective skills from experience in business, tech, and real estate, the couple and Canna Advisors found success within a few short months. Canna Advisors still operates today, guiding applicants through the state licensing process by ensuring all materials are of high quality and everything is filed correctly. Their team of consultants has successfully navigated the national and international cannabis regulatory space in 18 states, Puerto Rico, and Canada.

While being a mother in business—let alone the marijuana business—can come with some harsh stigma, Di does not fall victim to worrying what others think of her. She explains that, as a mother who has always worked in highly competitive fields with long and sometimes unpredictable hours, she "was never really part of the 'mom club'" and it does not seem to bother her. She elaborates; "I never felt any pressure or concern about what I did or how it would be perceived, but I *am* a rule follower!" Once she felt she could operate within the law, grey as it may have been, she was ready to charge onward. This courage is partly what makes Di such a force in the industry. Looking back, she feels strongly that her time spent as a young woman in the male dominated world of high tech prepared her well for the challenges she now faces in the cannabis realm. She has been supported by many women on her journey, and though she can obviously depend on Jay for support as both her husband and business partner, Di has not always been treated fairly by other male peers. To emphasize this, she shared a story from her days in the technology industry:

> The first company I worked for was a truly wonderful company—it was diverse and I am still very close to my former colleagues. Even still, I often felt there was a barrier for women to be outside salespeople. I am grateful for the mentors I had back then. One woman was especially influential to me. She was a very successful outside sales woman, and she was black. I understood then what she must have had to overcome to be successful. She was confident and she took me under her wing. She even worked with

her manager to help get me promoted, which is how I moved to Denver. However, when a hiring freeze wrecked my promotion, I was introduced to a new company and was hired for an outside sales position. The culture was very different—much more male dominated. I felt like I had to be 'one of the guys' to be accepted, which sometimes made me uncomfortable. There were countless occasions where inappropriate jokes were made or when I needed to thwart off unwanted advances. I remember one joke some of the men made about the word "harass" where they would constantly pronounce the word as "her-ass." There was another occasion where a VP slipped his hand into a chair I was about to sit in. I was also the only salesperson to get written up for not making my quota, even though my male counterparts weren't as well. I had so many barriers to fight through, but it made me determined to do better than them as a way of saying "fuck you!" And I did it, too! I went on to be the Regional Rep of the Year, got a Movado watch, went on a company paid trip to Egypt, and made more money that year than I ever have in my life.

For women considering exploring the cannabis frontier, Diane suggests that the industry not be taken lightly. "You always need to be thinking about how competitive it is and how important it is to stay ahead of the curve—always looking into the future." That said, when it comes to new women and fresh talent coming into the market, there are few women as encouraging as Di.

I want this to be, and continue to be, a diverse industry because I really love that about cannabis. I hope we can protect the collaborative, small community feel that we have now. The industry as a whole has the potential to be heavily influenced by women, specifically as it relates to health, helping people, social justice, and natural products—areas I find many women are passionate about.

Diane worries that many people entering the industry now see it purely as a money maker and assume financial success and industry knowledge will come easily. She cautions against this line of thinking, further explaining the many challenges faced by cannabis entrepreneurs. "As the market grows it's become more important for professionals in this space, especially women, to protect themselves with strong operating and/or partnership agreements."

She also acknowledges that, because of the perceived risk, a lot of seasoned business people did not move into cannabis right out of the gate. This may be part of the reason women were able to carve out niche roles and businesses for themselves early on, something that may have been more difficult had the market been flooded from the start.

> I think this gave women a better chance early on to get something started without the risk you feel in most industries of someone or another company coming in and taking over quickly. That said, I'm still not sure if it is easier for women to climb the ranks in cannabis. Many women I know and admire—about half a dozen of them right now—were pushed out or are in the process of being pushed out of businesses they started.

As a husband and wife team, Di offers a unique perspective on the industry. On one hand, there are few women as strong as Di in terms of negotiations or as it relates to management of a team and high level operations. But, on the other hand, she admits that there are clear benefits to having a male partner. "I know I can make sure my clients feel heard and cared for and I think women are generally better at building rapport and trust quickly. Sometimes, though, I know the meeting is going to be more successful if Jay takes over. There are men in our industry that, if they are going to talk business, they are more likely to talk to Jay first, then me."

To challenge these norms, Diane hopes that more organizations will rise up and acknowledge the importance of having an industry that is diverse.

> I would like to see The ArcView Group and Canopy Boulder [a business accelerator and venture fund in the cannabis industry]

continuing to promote female investors and entrepreneurs. I love the progress these two organizations have made and commend [them] for actively reaching out to recruit more women entrepreneurs and investors into the industry. I believe they will be part of the solution moving forward. And for the many people in the industry now, and the many more that will join, it is imperative that you participate [in promoting diversity].

Building an inclusive industry takes participation and determination from all sectors of the business and, like many women in cannabis, Diane hopes to see more people getting off the sidelines.

Diane continues to mentor entrepreneurs rising within cannabis. She is a founding member and benefactor of Women Grow, a founding member of the National Cannabis Industry Association, a lifetime and selection committee member of The ArcView Investment Group, a mentor for Canopy Boulder, and a sustaining member of both Americans for Safe Access and Students for Sensible Drug Policy. She is also a dedicated mother of three, and recently hired her 29-year-old son, Tyler, a six year industry veteran, as Director of Strategic Operations for Canna Advisors. "I was a mom when I was 20, so I've always had to mix working and family. It's not always easy, but I'm happy to have had that balance forced on me."

This February, Diane will celebrate her fiftieth birthday. "I feel like I've been in this industry for a long time! What's next for me? Probably setting up Canna Advisors in a way that will allow me to take things down a notch in the next five to seven years when I might consider being semi-retired. Maybe we will get acquired by a more traditional firm or be brought into something else. But I'll never fully retire," she laughs. In whichever direction Diane Czarkowski decides to pivot next, she will undoubtedly bring her immense talents and authentic passion.

———•———

Amy Dawn Bourlon-Hilterbran

FOUNDER OF AMERICAN MEDICAL
REFUGEES FOUNDATION
CEO OF MILLENNIUM GROWN
CREATOR OF THE TALK TO THE
6630507 HAND CAMPAIGN

"There's
just
no
stopping
a
mom."

AMY DAWN BOURLON-HILTERBRAN is a force to be reckoned with. A devoted mother and adoring wife, this former "small town girl" from Choctaw, Oklahoma, exudes a fierceness when she speaks; her voice is calm and rarely falters, but there is the feeling she could erupt into a roar at any moment. Amy has been faced with challenges and decisions no mother should have to face, and yet she continues onward in her mission, never considering the possibility of defeat. To Amy, being told "no" simply means "not yet." Her brainchild, the American Medical Refugees Foundation, has assisted over 200 struggling families—from 36 different states and 3 different countries—in gaining access to information, caregivers, medical marijuana insight, and medicine that is saving lives. Amy also serves as the Colorado State Chair for CannaMoms, a writer for MassRoots, the Regional Sales Manager for VeedVerks, and is a licensed Certified Nursing Assistant. Beyond that, Amy is highly regarded in the cannabis realm as a fierce advocate and activist for the full legalization of cannabis.

Amy, alongside her husband, Jason, and their family, relocated to Colorado so that their teenage son, Austin, could gain access to medical marijuana to treat the ravaging daily seizures he was suffering as a result of Dravet syndrome, a catastrophic form of epilepsy. Amy had campaigned to bring legalization of medical marijuana to Oklahoma but was unsuccessful. She recalls her feeling of desperation when there were no more viable options for treatment available in her home state: "When the doctors told us that there was nothing else that they could do, that the seizures would continue and the pharmaceutical drugs that were supposed to stop his seizures were shutting down [Austin's] organs; standing over my child as he lay on life support, I decided that was it." She told her husband, "He's dying. I can't just let our son die. We have to do something. I'm taking Austin to Colorado. You can come with me or not, but I'm going to try this plant." For six months, the family lived apart: Amy and Austin in Colorado, Jason and the younger children in Oklahoma, traveling back and forth to be together. When Jason saw the cannabis oils working, stopping his son's seizures, he resigned his position as a fireman in their hometown, packed up their truck, and moved himself and the younger boys permanently to Colorado.

When they had relocated their whole family to Florence, Colorado, Amy and Jason started weaning Austin off the medications that were shutting down his organs but not stopping his seizures—sometimes 19 or more pills each day. They introduced him to medical marijuana as a new daily regimen and form of treatment. "When we gave Austin his dose for the first time, he didn't have a seizure for three days so we knew it worked. Our child had dozens to hundreds of seizures daily, and we had three days without any after his first cannabis dose. There's just no denying that." Austin was soon experiencing 95% fewer seizures than he had been back home in Oklahoma. He could eat, walk, talk, and play more like a "normal" kid. Amy and Jason had hope again—they had their son back.

Though hopeful and relieved by Austin's immense improvement, Amy still remembers that, at times, she felt very lonely and overwhelmed. In Colorado she had "no support network at first, and it was very much a feeling of 'sink or swim.'" Beyond her feelings of isolation, Amy and Jason both grappled with the notion that "the first cannabis we legally gave our son, if we had done it one state away in our hometown, [we would] be considered felons."

Amy and Jason fretted over the other families struggling with this same problem that she knew had to be out there but were not able to relocate to other states. The thought of these people having to choose between treating their dying child or facing criminal charges haunted her. The pair transformed their feelings of discomfort and worry into action, and started the American Medical Refugees support group. It soon evolved into the American Medical Refugees Foundation (AMR) for which Amy and Jason recently filed nonprofit status. AMR has become an established network and foster community; a "family" for cannabis patients that highlights information, science, and data and gets these facts to the patients who need it most without propaganda and misinformation. A 'refugee,' in this case, is a person who has relocated from his/her home to be in a place where medical marijuana can be legally purchased and consumed.

AMR's mission is to bridge gaps in the stream of reliable information to help patients find the most effective methods of cannabis ingestion and treatment.

The early days of AMR were predictably challenging, made even more so by the fact that reaching out for support from her family back home was uniquely complicated. With palpable frustration in her voice, Amy explains that, to a certain degree, she feels she has had to protect them.

> We have a lot of family in Oklahoma and there's a lot of things I would like to share [with them] that I don't share because I don't want them to face the attention or the questions. We also have to be careful of the impact that our status or our statements have on families that are not in legal states. Guilt by association is very real in America.

Amy feels that, particularly when she first moved to Colorado, most of her family in Oklahoma was not able to witness Austin's improvement or acknowledge her work and achievements in a meaningful way. "While people believe you, they need to *see* it to really believe it. There's always critics—even when they see it—but just because you don't believe it, doesn't mean it isn't true. I never would have thought cannabis could save my child before—*never*—I was absolutely wrong. *I know this plant works.*" Amy is thankful that many people seem to "see it in a different light now," but adds that there are still those who will always be "critical." "People are so brain-trained to think that a pill and a pharmacist is better than a plant when it's actually quite the opposite."

Amy and her husband are both licensed medical professionals. Through her activism, Amy has seen the benefits of medical cannabis beyond the experiences of her own child. As it relates to the closed-minded naysayers who are ever present in the cannabis conversation, Amy asserts,

> People are over complicating what we used as a food, medicine, and a raw material source for hundreds of thousands of years. We

paid attention to our bodies, we paid attention to our children, and we responded. Now we want convenience. We want others to be responsible. The majority of the time when I interact with someone who is unwilling to listen to science and facts and doesn't care that seizures are going to kill my kid, I say, "I respect your right as an American to think the way you do—let us agree to disagree."

Her firm belief is that, "The one person that's going to create bad energy out of your passion, that's the person that is going to distract and exhaust you when you can use that same energy to teach and educate 20 other people. That one critic is just not ready yet." She lets out a laugh as she imparts a lesson brought with her from her home town: "Never argue with an idiot, they will drag you down to their level and beat you with experience every time."

Amy is as driven and persistent as anyone can be, but caring for a sick child while building AMR was not an easy feat. Her nearly ever-present laughter vanishes and she struggles to hold back tears as she reflects on the things her family, particularly Jason, has had to give up. "Moving from our friends and family has been a massive sacrifice." Her voice is practically a whisper as she reveals that, at times, she felt she would have to "choose between AMR and [her] family." She grew so tired of feeling like she was putting other families before her own, but then she would be reminded that "we are doing alright compared to many. There are people who are much worse off. I'm going to do all I can, while I can, when I can. It's the only way I'm going to know I lived right." There have been "very dark days" for Amy, but she has soldiered on for the sake of her values, guided by her unwavering moral convictions to patients and to the plant.

In September 2015, in the interest of raising funds to help more people and families as AMR continued to grow, Amy "threw her hat in the cannabis industry ring" and founded her company, Millennium Grown. In addition to blogs, broadcasts, and social media news campaigns, Millennium Grown hosts monthly, exclusive (you can't even buy a ticket) VIP events for hemp and cannabis industry leaders and business owners in Colorado. Deemed *the* VIP, Amy's private events feature "consumption friendly venues, high profile speakers and attendees; overall, a night filled with valuable information for industry leaders and business owners." Between the hype surrounding her events, AMR, other projects and campaigns, and her natural savvy for social media realness, Amy has developed a robust social media presence.

> It's been very organic—videos about our family and AMR have been seen tens of millions of times without any boosts or paid promotions. People are able to get information and hear us over the noise; we still don't quite understand why this happened to us, but we want our message to continue being authentic, genuine, and real; it's much like the plant—it'll find its way to get to the people.

A major reason Millennium Grown's social media platform has garnered so much attention is Amy's Talk to the 6630507 Hand Campaign. In August 2016, Amy started "the grassroots movement that is growing like a weed." It all began when she wrote "6630507" on her hand, representing the number of the US Government's patent that, according to an August 2016 *Cannabist* article entitled "Patent No. 6,630,507: Why the U.S. government holds a patent on cannabis plant compounds," the patent "covers the potential use of non-psychoactive cannabinoids—chemical compounds found within the plant species cannabis sativa—to protect the brain from damage or degeneration caused by certain diseases. [The patent] was granted to the U.S. Department of Health and Human Services in 2003." Under the Controlled Substance Act, the Drug Enforcement Administration (DEA) classifies drugs into five categories, known as schedules, rating each drug on its dependency potential and if it has any accepted medical use. These ratings range from Schedule I, representing drugs with the highest abuse potential and no currently accepted medical use, to Schedule V, representing many drugs that can be purchased at a pharmacy. Amy, and many others in the cannabis community, see this patent as revealing information about cannabis that is in direct conflict with its rating as a Schedule I drug.

I had been studying the patent for the past decade, and when my husband and I were watching TV and the DEA announced that they were not going to change the scheduling [of marijuana], I got up. I wrote the [patent] number on my hand and I took a photo with my cell, wrote a quick blurb about the hypocrisy and the legal basis for descheduling cannabis, and posted it to my personal Facebook page.

Her campaign worked immediately; it was viewed almost 10 million times from her personal page alone. "There are dozens of patents that prove cannabis is medicinal. *This* specific patent includes scientific evidence to show that cannabis is nonlethal—it disqualifies cannabis for all aspects as a controlled substance, proving cannabis should be removed completely from the Controlled Substance Act."

Amy says she created the photo and the post as a way to shine a spotlight on the deceit of the DEA and US government at large. "It was designed to call them out. I wanted real hands, real people, saying the same thing—Talk to the Hand, the 6630507 Hand." Spreading like wildfire, the internet blew up with pictures of thousands of hands from all over the world. These hand pictures, accompanied by personalized messages, flooded Facebook and Instagram. The Talk to the 6630507 Hand Campaign had gone viral and sparked global discussion on the DEA's decision to not reschedule or deschedule cannabis from the Controlled Substances Act. The campaign has generated "more Google searches for the patent number 6630507 than ever before in history." Activists, celebrities, socialites, musicians, politicians, doctors, lawyers, patients, and parents alike are flashing their hands by the thousands.

Aside from the obvious joy that comes from Austin's immense improvement and ability to live without pharmaceuticals, Amy acknowledges that "Talk to the 6630507 Hand" has developed into something "very special" and stands out as a highlight of her experience thus far in cannabis.

One of the really neat moments was when Willie Nelson participated in the campaign, when Woody Harrelson and Broken Lizard
participated in the campaign—when The History Channel, the
Washington Post, media on that level, and celebrities all across the
globe started reaching out—we knew our voices were being heard.
I was giddy. It was incredible. It felt like we had done a good job.
That was huge to us, getting the message to the most people. We
get to see the hundreds of patients here in Colorado, but we know
how many more there are. It was pretty unbelievable to hear from
so many people are out there. [Talk to the 6630507 Hand] went
global and it got people talking. It has people correcting others,
educating others, and we are a little overwhelmed by how compassionate people can be. People want to do the right thing.

She stresses that, in order for a major shift to happen, "leaders need to be
more educated, citizens need to be more informed. People have been without this knowledge for so long, fear still has us living in *Reefer Madness*;
people are uncomfortable talking about this plant and thinking of it as
medicine." Amy goes on:

This is America in 2017. It is our right to choose what we consume. Whether it's a choice to consume medically or wanting to
consume the only nonlethal recreational drug on the planet—it
is our choice. We should not have to defend those rights. Those
inalienable rights, those constitutional rights to life, liberty, and
the pursuit of happiness were paid for many, many years ago. Even
now, our soldiers and veterans pay the cost for us every single day.

Many of the marijuana medical refugees Amy works with are veterans
seeking treatment for PTSD, combat injuries, and other conditions related to their service. She is a committed voice for veterans. Amy burst
out, "I don't understand any American who would deny a veteran the
right to choose a plant. It's a travesty. It's hideous. If anyone has earned

the right to choose—the veterans have certainly earned it." And many agree. According to a *Cannabist* article published on January 30, 2017, entitled "Bill adding PTSD to Colorado medical marijuana list clears Senate committee," the state "Senate committee voted 5-0 to advance a bill that seeks to include PTSD as a qualifying condition for medical marijuana in Colorado." This bill, co-sponsored by Senator Irene Aguilar (D-Denver) and Rep. Jonathan Singer, D-Longmont, "would add PTSD and acute stress disorder as "disabling medical conditions" under the state [of Colorado's] medical marijuana law."

From Amy's perspective, veterans and children are the "heartstrings" of the cannabis movement. "It's the kids and vets that will change a lot of people's perceptions." Amy also feels that movement and change should start at home. In order for people to learn the truth and shift the conversation, she believes "we have to lead from within. It starts in the home. It's not the leadership that's going to determine this great country, it's our citizens. It starts at the local level and it starts within our homes, talking to our kids, instilling common sense and compassion again." She elaborates, "People think pills are okay—they think they're safe, legal, the best choice." Meanwhile, Amy estimates that the vast majority of veteran suicides each day happen to veterans who have either tried prescription drugs for their conditions or are currently using them. According to the US Department of Veterans Affairs' 2016 study, there were an average of 20 veteran suicides per day in 2014. Amy hopes that, as cannabis legalization continues to prevail in more and more states, we see a dramatic decline in both veteran suicides and prescription drug use.

Amy's wealth of knowledge was acquired by necessity. When she was searching for solutions for Austin and in the early days of AMR, she credits more than a handful of caregivers and leaders with helping her acquire imperative information. She emphasizes the number of women who contributed to her personal education in the field.

The key people that helped me find information and connect with others were women I met in the movement and industry. They were mothers, nurses, doctors, and seekers of knowledge looking to help their kids. I've never seen something so fierce. When in other industries and arenas you see women who are hypercompetitive and driven, unwilling to assist, our industry is full of women who want me to succeed, who care about me and my family, my dreams and my goals.

She begins to get emotional: "I am humbled and honored to be surrounded by some of the most amazing women on the planet." She relates a story of how one particular woman aided and inspired her:

> When we were still in Oklahoma, I had support from this amazing woman, Julie Hutchison. She is the founder of the Chelsea Hutchison Foundation (CHF), named after her daughter who died of SUDEP [Sudden Unexplained Death in Epilepsy Patients]. The CHF provides seizure dogs and monitors to those in need and sends families to Disneyland every year. When we got to Colorado and I was able to meet her, she took me under her wing, she became a friend, regardless of the fact that my son was now a cannabis patient. To her, it didn't matter what medicine he was taking, all she cares about is the patient and their improvement.

To Amy, this was absolutely refreshing, especially after everything she had gone through in leaving her home state. She told us that it is unfortunately common for many organizations and foundations to discriminate against patients choosing "controversial" medical paths like cannabis treatments, so for Julie to embrace her and AMR was profound. "This woman refused to let anything stand in the way of her patients' care and support. I have seen great leadership by men in this industry, that is for sure, but I have seen no greater leadership than by the women in this industry and movement. They aren't just thinking about the industry, but about the patients as well." She sighs and proclaims, *"There's just no stopping a mom."*

Amy doesn't hesitate to say that it was primarily women who provided her with most of the information and support she needed to help others through Millennium Grown and AMR. Coming into cannabis from the sphere of advocacy and activism, she offers an interesting perspective on the grass ceiling and how she felt inspired to enter the industry sector. "I've seen the boys club in other industries, and I saw the cannabis industry and these amazing females that did not seem hindered by their gender. I wanted to be a part of that." Amy felt that she would be a good example of leadership in this space because she "represented the professionalism, but also the personal side, the patient." Since her entry into this industry, she has grown to feel "very proud of what [the industry has] become. I believe it's the only industry with a level playing field for women, and I believe it's a very righteous journey where you can prosper financially while working to provide medicine to the people who truly need it. We are all in this together. Gender is just like race—*it doesn't matter.* It matters who you are and what you are trying to do."

Amy keeps her advice to women who may be looking to get involved in cannabis simple: "Keep it classy and stay professional. Use your brain. Be respectful. Work hard. Tell the truth and do all you can. It's the 'basics,' that's all it takes—but most people won't do what it takes. It's just the right thing to do. When you know it's right, you just have to do it." And she has done so much. With Talk to the 6630507 Hand Campaign, Amy created a sustainable campaign that has reached hundreds of millions of people all over the world. She overcame struggles with her family and with her son's illness only to turn around and offer support to others in need. She is a remarkably strong woman, but she says, "I don't think I'm special, *I'm just a part of something special.*" She wants to see other women join her in her work and hopes the stories collected in this book will "inspire" some to take a leap of faith and offer their talents to the cannabis industry and movement.

Looking ahead, Amy Dawn Bourlon-Hilterbran will continue as CEO of Millennium Grown and creator of the Talk to the 6630507 Hand Campaign, but will designate other leadership for AMR, serving on the board and as a prominent figurehead while releasing the reins as it expands with additional state chapters. Amy will continue to work out of her small office in downtown Denver as she waits for her larger space to fall in line this year. Boasting a rooftop venue, her office, Depot MetLo, is "the perfect setting" to kick off her 2017 plan. "I want to focus on events and getting the platform on social media out to the masses. This venue in Denver and others like it in legal states are perfect to propel my business plan while educating people on the plant." Amy also plans to "implement change at local levels and educate city council members in states where cannabis is legal, where states are limiting plant counts, restricting patient access—where local leadership is practicing medicine without a license, there needs to be legal recourse."

Amy says the best way to implement change is by starting new state chapters of AMR, which currently has chapters in Colorado, California, and New Mexico and will soon be found in Texas, Oregon, Washington, and Florida. "One of our missions is to make sure that our refugees remain politically active in *their* state or country so that laws can change so that, eventually, they can go home. Some states will take longer than others." Her son Austin, she beams, "is doing amazing! He is fully weaned off of the pharmaceuticals that were shutting down his organs. There are no more indicators of damage to his kidneys or liver. He has days and weeks now with no seizures at all! He is talking more, singing and playing, and is truly healthier and happier—we all are." She adds, "It's going to be a huge year."

Dr. Sue Sisley

PRESIDENT AND PRINCIPAL INVESTIGATOR
AT SCOTTSDALE RESEARCH INSTITUTE

"I don't want to be labeled as an activist . . .

I am a scientist

looking for real answers. I want to know the true objective data about the medicinal benefits of cannabis."

DR. SUE SISLEY is an Arizona-based MD who practices internal medicine and psychiatry. For decades, Sue has been committed to her patients and has a special place in her heart for the many veterans she has treated throughout her practice. Sue deeply respects veterans for their contributions to our country and feels strongly that it is her duty to care for them in the most effective and beneficial way, especially the veterans suffering from military-related medical issues such as PTSD. As she looks back on her story and journey into cannabis, it is not surprising that the people she feels such compassion for as a doctor were the same people who shifted her feelings about medical marijuana.

A self-described "staunch Republican" from Arizona, Sue is not your average cannabis activist. In fact, she is still surprised—and also somewhat bothered by the activist label.

> People refer to me as an activist, but I was forced to become one. When I learned of the myriad of ways the government was systematically impeding cannabis research, I felt it was my duty to expose this wrongdoing. Also, I was one of a handful of credible doctors and scientific researchers that was urging legalization of medical cannabis in Arizona. I don't want to be labeled as an activist but, instead, as an advocate for rigorous research; I am a scientist looking for real answers. I want to know the true objective data about medicinal benefits of cannabis, as well as the risks.

Sue's evolution from a conservative practicing physician and cannabis skeptic to a nationally recognized cannabis researcher, one who acts as a Chief Medical Director for 14 licensed marijuana businesses from Pennsylvania to Hawaii, did *not* happen overnight. While she never ceased to provide exemplary medical care, it took years of ailing patients coming into her office and sharing their experiences with marijuana for Sue's opinions to eventually soften. Over time, more and more of Sue's patients, specifically veterans, informed her that they were not going to continue taking their prescription medications and that they had instead turned to cannabis. "Most were sharing that cannabis was much more beneficial to them as opposed to the medications I had been prescribing. I was highly judgmental and dismissive of their claims at first, but they trusted me and continued to share their stories, never giving up on me." Her patients' perseverance resulted in Sue's eventual reconsideration. While anecdotal in nature, Sue eventually heard too many compelling reports to dismiss the potential of medical marijuana.

> I had a few patients who were very conservative and who had never demonstrated any kind of drug-seeking behavior. They were high functioning, had families and full-time jobs, and were certainly not the types of people you would suspect to be using cannabis. A few of these patients went as far as having a child or spouse join them for an appointment with me. I remember a child once saying, "I got my dad back," and that was it—over time, stories like this wore down my skepticism and it became impossible to ignore what they were saying.

Sue maintains that she is not pro-cannabis, she is pro-science and socially Libertarian. This is why, when Arizona's medical marijuana ballot initiative came about, she felt it was her responsibility to support it. "[Arizona] had already gotten [medical marijuana] approved before, but it hadn't stuck. I felt 2010 was our time, but also felt compelled to get involved because there were no other physicians willing to go on record for this." Sue's participation, alongside other cannabis activists, led to the passing of Arizona Proposition 203 and the creation of a legal medical marijuana program in Arizona. She was now being sought out by patients all over the state and she recalls feeling like her decision to support the ballot initiative "crystallized her involvement in [the] cannabis movement." She had also become more aware of cannabis as a social justice issue and mentions, "I found myself frustrated by the actions of our government; especially racial disparities in the enforcement of drug laws—there is such an immense unfairness when a system wastes millions of taxpayer dollars by throwing people in cages over this plant."

Her mind irreversibly opened, Sue began to look for any data or research she could find relating to marijuana. She remembers finding controlled trials written up in various peer-reviewed medical journals, but recognized immediately that the trials were very limited or underpowered.

> People are always saying it's so hard to do a real cannabis medical study, but that's not all true. What's challenging is getting a cannabis clinical trial approved in US when your goal is to research medical cannabis efficacy. Many studies have been conducted over the past few decades throughout the US, but the vast majority are examining safety issues—focused on documenting harmful side effects of cannabis or the likelihood of addiction to cannabis, but not evaluating both safety and efficacy.

As a former skeptic, Sue also felt that states like Arizona were slow to accept marijuana as an alternative medicine *because* there was not much rigorous research to defend that position.

Sue's family and close friends were, predictably, surprised by her decision to research and explore the potential of medical cannabis. She had never been a cannabis user and her conservative reputation left some people rattled by her gradual change of heart on the issue. But Sue takes care to always balance her personal views with her view as a scientist. She explains, "This plant is far less toxic than many of the medications I prescribe every day and it is being unfairly vilified." She goes on to share that she "knows I've raised some eyebrows and that some people thought I became a 'stoner,' but I still haven't tried it." Sue sees no need to consume and wants to approach her research without bias. "I'm healthy right now and don't need it as a medicine. If I were sick, or suffering from something where cannabis could help me—different story. But for now, I would rather approach my scientific studies without any preconceived notions."

Sue admits that she has had moments where she wondered if she had been "swept up into the cannabis movement," given how much time she spends around supporters who "believe there is a major conspiracy against cannabis policy reform due to intensive lobbying from powerful groups like Big

Pharma, law enforcement," and more. She shared that she routinely spends time questioning her own objectivity, but consistently comes back to the same answer: "I only care about collecting objective data that is unassailable and, ultimately, getting it published in peer-reviewed medical journals." She firmly believes that irrefutable evidence of marijuana's efficacy, weighed against its risks, is the only avenue to shifting the public thinking on marijuana.

If the evidence is solid, it will prove that more testing and clinical research is necessary to fully explore the medical possibilities of cannabis. "I would love to see [our team] uncover new treatments for PTSD as a result of my trial, but I know we might find something else. Some of my patients report negative responses to cannabis and remember feeling paranoid or anxious." Sue explains that the varying reactions are likely in direct correlation to each individual phenotype of the cannabis plant and shares that, down the road, someone will need to begin studying specific genetics so the way cannabis is prescribed may be tailored to treat specific ailments. "Marijuana is not *one* plant; there are hundreds of unique phenotypes. One strain may cause paranoia in a particular patient, but a different strain may help them cope with PTSD." Sue is a scientist through and through, and she works hard every day to ensure the integrity of her studies by remaining unbiased amongst the growing community of cannabis supporters.

Sue continues to serve as a doctor of internal medicine, but has dedicated an enormous amount of time to her marijuana research, a pursuit that was not easy. "We hit one roadblock after another after another," she remembers. In 2009, Sue was invited to partner with MAPS, the Multidisciplinary Association for Psychedelic Studies. According to MAPS' website, www.maps.org, MAPS was founded in 1996 and is "a 501(c)(3) nonprofit research and educational organization that develops medical, legal, and cultural contexts for people to benefit from the careful uses of psychedelics and marijuana." Sue describes her collaboration with MAPS as "heavenly," and has come to cherish the people who run the organization as lifelong friends and colleagues who are working towards similar objectives. Once linked with MAPS, Sue began serving as the principal investigator of a crucial cannabis efficacy study which obtained FDA approval in 2011. Sue also followed all of the processes outlined by the University of Arizona (U of A), where she was employed, as it related to obtaining internal review board (IRB) approval. The roadblocks felt more daunting when they came from an unlikely source, Sue's own university:

> I was a part of the University of Arizona community for a long time. I went to med school there myself and, after, became part of the clinical faculty. After the initiative passed, I began leading the study through the university's internal review board process. I was thrilled to learn that we were granted IRB approval in 2012, but the top university administrators—unfortunately—did not share my enthusiasm. They found every reason to obstruct our work. I became at odds with my own university administration, a university that I loved. I was always pro-U of A, but none of that matters when leadership is adversarial towards your research. [The president] felt my research would be harmful to the school's brand . . . she didn't want the optics of veterans smoking pot on campus and she fought me every step of the way. I remember, at one point, the VP of health sciences telling me that the university couldn't allow me to get started because there were no office [or] lab spaces available. I promptly found an entire wing of unused office spaces, but it wasn't going to make a difference. They weren't going to support this type of cannabis efficacy research which, they felt, could harm their ability to draw down millions of federal dollars annually. Their view was that the study had to be blocked to protect federal grant funding.

Given that Sue was nontenured, the university had the power to fire her; however, administrators made the more strategic decision to, simultaneously, not renew any of her three contracts. She was terminated by the University of Arizona in June 2014, receiving three letters of nonrenewal indicating that she would be stripped of all her contracts at five o'clock that Friday. Sue was, and continues to be, a Wildcat for life and has tremendous respect for the hardworking students, faculty, and staff who work in the

trenches to make the University of Arizona thrive. While she expresses
that leaving the university was not an easy time in her life, Sue chose to
focus on the positive—primarily that her exit put a national spotlight on
the barriers to cannabis efficacy research, garnered outrage at her uncer-
emonious separation from her alma mater, and raised widespread awareness of political attacks on scientific freedom.

> We got worldwide media coverage because it was so mystifying to
> everyone that a doctor possessing a fully funded study *with FDA
> and university IRB approval* would be removed in this way. The
> study received over a full year of media coverage because of this,
> but, most importantly, gained a partnership with Johns Hopkins
> University in Baltimore [that] agreed to serve as a second study
> site for the protocol. And the state of Colorado offered us a $2.1
> million grant to continue the trial—the first government money
> MAPS had ever received for cannabis research.

With funding and strong collaborators from Johns Hopkins, the University
of Colorado Denver, and the University of Pennsylvania, Sue was well
positioned to launch the study and proceeded to assemble her team. Her
role as site principal investigator for the only FDA approved, randomized,
controlled trial in the world is a massive deal. The study seeks to examine
the safety and efficacy of whole plant marijuana in combat veterans with
treatment-resistant PTSD. This study is supremely relevant as diagnosed
cases of PTSD continue to rise but few effective treatment options exist.
However, true to character, Sue did not let herself get carried away by the
excitement of the grant from Colorado or by the national media attention
the study had received; she anticipated more hurdles ahead—and she was
right. Being let go from the University of Arizona was certainly one of her
first major obstacles, but debating with the DEA and FDA would prove to
be far more challenging in nature.

Sue is continually beating the odds. As a woman working in the cannabis domain as well as in her career as a scientist, she has encountered

many unexpected barriers. By working to break through the glass ceiling in science, a field overwhelmingly dominated by men, and by pursuing highly controversial marijuana research, Sue certainly challenges the stereotype of what a woman can achieve.

First of all, female scientists in general are rare to see, and when you see them, they are rarely challenging authority—i.e. they don't get in the face of administration or confront higher-ups—but they usually don't have to. But if you take on a subject matter like cannabis, you immediately have a target on your back. I was never impolite, always very measured and careful and respectful to everybody, but I wasn't a timid shrinking violet, either, and I think that was a problem for me. I believe there are members of our legislature who believe women should fulfill very traditional roles. Females who are strident and fearless pose an even bigger threat to that administration. In my experience, they would view my behavior as aggressive but I viewed it as assertive in defending my field of study. This was an FDA approved project, not 10 stoners on a couch saying: let's study cannabis.

Some members of the Arizona legislature labeled Sue the pied piper of the cannabis movement after her work on Arizona's medical marijuana ballot initiative that helped lead to its passing. She feels this was a deliberate attempt to dilute her reputation as an objective scientist by associating her with the activist agenda.

Many of these prohibitionists don't believe in science. They believe that most cannabis research is just pseudoscience, rigged to make cannabis look favorable. In order to combat their outdated thinking, I need to prove to the public I'm *not* an activist. I'm an *advocate* for research over politics, and hope other elected officials agree that research should never be handcuffed by politics. But I'm not pro-cannabis—I'm pro-science.

Sue's work on cannabis in the name of science reaches beyond her work with Johns Hopkins. She is a member of the faculty at Colorado State University (CSU) and was recruited as a member of the core planning team to organize CSU's Institute of Cannabis Research in Pueblo, Colorado. For the past two years, she has also been an active member of the Nevada ILAC Medical Cannabis Commission where she has outlined regulations for laboratory testing, including limits on pesticides, residual solvents, and other guidelines that are currently being used as a model for other states' medical cannabis laws. She is also a member of the steering committee at Thomas Jefferson University. With much to keep her busy, Sue does not allow herself to be distracted; she never take her eyes off of the prize.

> Long term, I want to help MAPS put whole plant cannabis through the entire FDA process. Additionally, I want to continue fighting for access to better quality and varieties of cannabis study drugs to be used for controlled trials. There is currently a government-enforced monopoly in the US to obtain cannabis for research purposes. This NIDA [contract with the] University of Mississippi has had no competition for 48 years—and this is unlike any other Schedule I substance where there are numerous labs supplying study drugs. This has to change.

Many people may find themselves surprised to learn that, while cannabis study drugs are limited and difficult to obtain, scientists nationwide can, with relative ease, procure LSD, mushrooms, and MDMA in the form of purified study drug from numerous research labs across the United States. There is no monopoly on the supply of other Schedule I drugs; only the least toxic of all Schedule I drugs, cannabis, is forced to struggle with this monopoly. Due, in part, to two decades of lobbying by Sue's team at MAPS, the DEA recently announced in the summer of 2016 that they would be accepting applications for new research growers. Sue notes that this announcement was not accompanied by a timeline and that, without proper pressure, the DEA will most likely drag its feet on making this decision, resulting in the continuation of the NIDA monopoly and, consequently, limited availability to cannabis study drugs. Sue has decided to apply for a Schedule I license as a bulk manufacturer, and is confident that she will receive strong consideration because she is a researcher who already possesses the license permitting her to study and handle clinical-grade Schedule I substances. "It's now a waiting game," she says with a long sigh.

With years of battle (and science) under her belt, one might think that Sue is interested in passing the torch to new researchers. While she absolutely encourages women to join this sector, she isn't going anywhere anytime soon.

> For the last 10 years, we have been trying to eliminate the barriers to cannabis research so that scientists from all walks of life can participate in this work. As an example, we had to go through a three year public health review and then spent another year proving to the government that this three year process was unnecessary and redundant. The Obama administration announced they were ending the PHS review last year, and while these stories don't always get picked up, they are critically important to future researchers. I think that, while my firing helped to catapult our story, it had a chilling effect on researchers nationally who may now be afraid to pursue this cannabis efficacy research. My goal is to cut through the red tape so that this will be a more welcoming environment for future scientists. Now is the time for researchers to start considering this . . . no one is in an ivory tower; all of us want to mentor young scientists and I know I will need to continue identifying talented scientists who demonstrate the patience [and] perseverance to overcome government stonewalling.

Sue Sisley has an enormous arsenal of work to be proud of, but getting her to acknowledge her own accomplishments can sometimes be a challenge; her humility never fades. When pushed, however, Sue shared an accomplishment that she considers to be one of her greatest victories. As she reflects on her exit from the University of Arizona, her time spent advocating for Arizona's Proposition 203, and her outspoken dialogue surrounding the DEA cannabis research monopoly, Sue identifies a common trend: "My proudest moments and professional achievements have been the times I stood up to the bullies," an effort that will most definitely pave the way for many brilliant scientists in the future.

Genifer Murray

FOUNDER OF CARBON BLUE
FOUNDER OF GENIFER M. CANNABIS INSPIRED JEWELRY

"We need and want
new women
to come in,
breathe life into us,
and carry the torches forward."

SCIENCE AND LUXURY jewelry—not a pairing most would make. However, in Genifer Murray's case, these two interests fuse together beautifully as she moves into a new phase of her career within the cannabis industry. Genifer holds a Bachelor's degree in microbiology and has always been passionate about science. She is also the daughter of a jewelry maker and gemologist and has a deep appreciation for her father's impressive knowledge of that business. "Not all jewelry is created equal *and* not all cannabis is created equal," has become her new mantra. It should come as no surprise that, given these interests, Genifer owns and operates a scientific lab consulting business, Carbon Blue Consulting, and co-owns a brand new cannabis jewelry line called GENIFER M Cannabis Inspired Jewelry with her father. "Carbon Blue is my passion for science brought to life, but the jewelry has very organically become a catalyst in sparking the conversation about cannabis with many people I meet outside of the industry; a non-threatening way to ask me about this amazing plant."

Genifer is a fifth generation Colorado native who has been in the cannabis industry since the early days in 2010. While she was educated in science, she spent the first chapter of her career in sales, and remembers feeling like nothing "blew [her] socks off." Genifer grew up in Colorado but decided to move to Arizona in 2004 to spend time with her father, with whom she didn't grow up. "I needed a change and was looking for new opportunities. I decided not to stay [in Arizona] and moved back to Colorado in 2009." Genifer returned to Arizona frequently to visit her father and, on one of these visits, had a conversation that changed her future entirely.

> While visiting my father and dining at a friend's restaurant, that I started talking to a guy who was sitting near the bar. We got to chatting and I shared that I had a background in science and the guy perked up. He asked me a question that got my wheels turning: "What do you think about testing marijuana?" I had no idea what that meant so I asked and he said, "Like pharmaceutical companies test their products for the active ingredients."

This was the "huge light bulb moment" that would inspire Genifer to develop CannLabs, one of the first independent marijuana testing laboratories in Colorado. Independent testing laboratories conduct scientific testing on cannabis flower and marijuana infused products, resulting in greater product consistency. Genifer recalls her excitement and fear, feelings that often accompany an illuminating moment of discovery, especially in cannabis:

> I remember thinking: I could go to jail! The first time I called the Department of Regulatory Agencies to ask a series of questions they scared me to death! I remember thinking that, because I don't have a husband or kids or anything, I didn't have as much to lose as many of my peers, but I was still afraid of winding up in prison.

Despite her initial trepidation, Genifer decided to move forward with her idea, posting on Facebook that she owned a lab in the cannabis industry. The positive responses she received from her family and friends surprised her, and Genifer relied heavily on that support during the tough times that were in store for CannLabs.

The person Genifer coincidentally met at her friend's bar was, in fact, a small business owner from Colorado Springs, CO. They continued discussing the concept of a "testing lab," and, after several meetings and lengthy conversations, the two founded CannLabs. Genifer remembers driving all over the state during CannLabs' early days, desperately trying to convince marijuana businesses of the importance of testing their products through an independent laboratory. At the end of 2011, she bought out her partner and brought on a new one in hopes that this would improve business. "I cold called, I drove my butt everywhere, but we were really struggling. Testing wasn't a requirement at this time, nor was there a license for testing, and people really weren't that interested in spending the money or time on cannabis testing." At the beginning of fall 2012, they were thinking about shutting down the lab.

That all changed with the 2012 election when Amendment 64 passed, ending prohibition in Colorado, an effort to which Genifer contributed through her work on the Governor's Implementation Task Force. Colorado's state website "colorado.gov" published a report on March 13, 2013 explaining the Task Force, established by Governor Hickenlooper, and its purpose. "The Task Force was assembled to assist the state and local governments in the process of implementing the new law by proposing a regulatory framework that [promoted] the health and safety of the people of Colorado."

When Amendment 64 passed, Genifer realized she had a legitimate business model because the amendment called for mandatory testing of all cannabis products. Genifer and her partner had "bootstrapped the business," and needed money to ramp up their operation to take on mandatory testing. They started looking for investment funds in the summer of 2013, but found that "there wasn't any money at that time, not even hard money loans." They began to be approached by companies that wanted to take CannLabs public, but it wasn't until April 2014 that they found their investor, executed a reverse merger, and became a publicly traded company.

Business surged; CannLabs quickly grew from five employees to more than 40. However, toward the end of 2014, Genifer noticed some strange and unexpected things happening within her business. Admittedly, this is where she made her gravest mistake; one that, to this day, she speaks about in a measured tone intended to educate others so they may benefit from her misfortune.

I trusted my business partner with the investment side of the company—paperwork, managing our books, etc. These areas are not my strengths, especially the contract side. I also trusted the investor, the board, and our new CEO. Looking back, I should have had my own attorney working for me, not just one for the business, to make sure that I—Genifer, the person—was protected. This was just one of the mistakes that resulted in my losing CannLabs. You always have to have [an attorney] that you trust looking after you unless you are the sole owner of the business. . . . I think women tend to be more trusting and it can get us into trouble if we do not have legal support. So what I tell all women I speak with now

[is]: the first thing you need to do is find a lawyer and the second thing you need to do is find an accountant. Have these professionals involved in setting up the business structure and all paperwork and, most importantly, make sure you understand the documents! Don't be embarrassed to ask questions. It is imperative that you understand *every single thing* on the paper.

She shifts gears and it becomes clear that, while Genifer is willing to share her story, primarily to protect and caution other women, she has moved on and put this painful experience behind her.

Losing CannLabs was the hardest thing I've been through. I felt like I had lost everything. I didn't date for nearly six years because I poured all of my time and energy into the business. My entire life had been CannLabs. After A64, when business started to skyrocket, I never thought for one second that [the company] wouldn't make it. I remember when I was locked out of my business in September of 2015 and that time was extremely difficult.

What makes Genifer incredibly special as both a businesswoman and a cannabis industry pioneer is how she handled herself after the lockout. Genifer, ever resilient, did not retreat quietly in defeat. When asked to describe the timeframe between losing CannLabs and launching Carbon Blue she enthusiastically stated that her new company was up and running in October 2015, not even a full month after she was closed out of CannLabs.

With Carbon Blue Consulting on the docket and a seriously strong network of people encouraging her to plow onward, Genifer began putting her life back in order—this time with a more concrete understanding about *how* to safely build a business without letting it define her entire life. "There are so many opportunities out there—if things don't work out the first time, get creative! Try again! Do what you love." Carbon Blue is everything Genifer once loved about her first company: working with microbiologists and chemists; designing and building lab testing facilities around the country; and, of course, science. She has not yet started marketing the business, yet still has plenty of clients with all of her current leads coming in from referrals.

> So many people lifted me up to help get this business going. . . . I remember getting messages from colleagues of mine, including a message of support from one of my former competitors. All of this made me realize what being a pioneer really means: it's about the relationships that you build and keep. The foundation is built on relationships. The first time I met all of these people, we were growing our businesses side by side. That is something no one else will have an opportunity to do because these new industries only come around every so often. Regardless of whether I like someone or not, or if they like me or not, there is a mutual respect between us for growing our companies at the same time.

Genifer expresses deep appreciation for the women who were—literally—growing their businesses alongside hers.

> Julie Dooley, Jill Lamoureux, Betty Aldworth, Kristi Kelly, Barb Visher, Christie Lunsford, Di Czarkowski, Meg Sanders, Amy Dilullo, Jan Cole, Jaime Lewis—all of us have been around for some time and have been there for each other and supported one another. It is because of these women that I am able to be where I am today.

Despite everything she went through with CannLabs, Genifer still affirms, "It truly is the best thing I have ever done. I wouldn't change it." Would things have been easier for her if she had waited on the sidelines for a few years instead of diving headfirst into the uncharted cannabis waters? Maybe. But then, she didn't get into this industry because it was going to be easy. "We are so lucky that we get to pave the way. We get to form this thing. It takes everybody: business owner, activist, non-profit—all of us, not one or the other. If we can get on the same page and realize we can all be in this together, working together, the industry will thrive."

As Genifer reflected on some of her fondest memories and favorite people she has come across in cannabis, it is patients that come to her mind before all else.

> I'll never forget Charlotte Figi, the now famous little girl who has Dravet syndrome and was saved by cannabis oil. I will also hold dear the first patient I ever met who has remained near and dear to my heart. Her name was Fran and she was this little four foot ten, 69-year-old firecracker. Those who know me know that I ask almost everyone I come across what they think about cannabis. When I asked [Fran] for her perspective, she opened up to me and confided that she had been considering taking her own life because she was in such intense pain. She had tried so many pain medications and nothing was working for her. It was actually her son who suggested she try cannabis.

Genifer was able to link Fran up with a medical marijuana dispensary close to her home. Guiding the older woman through the process of finding medicine that brought her lifesaving relief is a deeply personal hallmark of Gen's career. Charlotte Figi's condition, Dravet syndrome, is a rare and severe form of intractable epilepsy. According to a 2013 CNN article about Charlotte, "Intractable means that the seizures are not controlled by medication."[1] Around the time Genifer met Charlotte and Fran, she also met Dr. Sanjay Gupta and introduced him to The Stanley Brothers, a group of siblings who have become famous for co-founding the "Realm of Caring Foundation" and creating Charlotte's Web, a high CBD strain of cannabis named after Charlotte Figi.

> [Dr. Sanjay Gupta] was absolutely skeptical of cannabis when I met him in 2013. I remember speaking with him and [his show's]

producers and, while they were all so kind, I could tell that they had a long way to go before they would believe in the medical properties of cannabis. At the time, I wasn't operating out of our lab—we were in a temporary space waiting for our lab to be finished and licensed. So I know when he and his producers first came to meet me, they were likely unimpressed by our facility compared to all of the other major, standard style, non-cannabis labs he had seen and worked in before. He was such a sweet man and I am so fortunate to have met him and am so proud of him and his team for coming into cannabis at that time with an open mind and for agreeing to meet with The Stanley Brothers and others in the industry.

Genifer's commitment to cannabis patients remains intact today; she currently serves on the board of The Flowering H.O.P.E. Foundation, founded by Jason Cranford. The foundation works to "facilitate safe access to life changing medicines"[2] for those suffering from a wide array of conditions. Genifer is proud of the entire team's efforts to help the sick obtain medical cannabis.

Genifer's future sparkles, just the way she does when she shares the many hardships she has gracefully weathered and triumphs she has achieved during her seven years in the industry. GENIFER M. Jewelry, which launched in late 2016, has taken off and women throughout the cannabis industry—and beyond—are flaunting her gorgeous designs. (Genifer wears her staple piece in her photo.) Genifer won't be satisfied until her pieces hit the mainstream marketplace and she sees people everywhere wearing "the jewelry that makes a difference." She gleams, "I want to make jewelry that symbolizes the end of prohibition. Jewelry that sparks conversation about cannabis. I want these pieces to help send a message to people outside of our industry." She intends to run both GENIFER M. Jewelry and Carbon Blue Consulting simultaneously and will continue sharing her personal story. Genifer is a frequent panelist and speaker at conferences and educational events around the country, and was even selected to lecture at the University of Colorado on the importance of cannabis testing.

She exhibits compassion and a genuine willingness to educate others, even if it means she must relive some of the pain from her past.

> This industry is important for driven women. Look at all of us—we are all so different and we've been able to do this. We can go to younger ladies and encourage them and guide them. I can help people so they don't have to go through the pains that I did. We should be helping other young women come on board. It has been hard being a pioneer and we need and *want* new women to come in, breathe life into us, and carry the torches forward. The more we talk about it, the better off other women will be.
>
> I think one of my highlights has been speaking at the Women Grow Leadership Summit—getting up there to speak about the mistakes I made, to everyone else, I learned that [my words and story] made a difference in other people's lives. I heard from so many women via social media and email. They shared that my presentation drove them to hire an attorney, or reread their operating agreements, or reconsider a reverse merger, etc. and that they were so thankful I was willing to share my story.

Genifer truly exemplifies what she hopes to see throughout the industry as it grows, and is a shining example of resilience in the face of adversity. She has watched the industry change and evolve and is a true supporter of the activists who started this movement. "Activism gave way to business which gave way to industry, and we need to pay homage to those people who were there working tirelessly from the beginning." When she says that she is eager to help new women join the industry, she means it. She is an open book and an incredible resource for female entrepreneurs. To anyone coming into the future of cannabis she implores,

> Stay true to yourself and your morals. Through all of this, I have stayed honest, remained a champion for health and safety, and I have never stopped advocating for the end users—the patients. I

am proud that I have held true to that. I am driven by a pay-it-forward philosophy toward the industry's next generation of women."

Moving forward, Genifer Murray would like to be part of instituting a universal standard for testing labs, which would hold businesses, large and small, accountable for implementing quality control processes—a goal that will ultimately help patients feel comfortable that the marijuana they consume is safe and consistent. Gen exclaims, "Science! Truly, I love it! I love to teach people and educate people; I have taught the *Testing Crash Course* countless times at MJ Business Daily and, every single time, I am so happy. I love seeing all the eager new faces." Genifer also looks forward to the success of her jewelry line and spreading the word of cannabis in a different way: "Wearing it and using it as a conversation starter to change the perception of a professional woman who smokes cannabis."

———

Notes

1. "Marijuana Stops Child's Severe Seizures," Saundra Young, *CNN*, August 7, 2013, http://www.cnn.com/2013/08/07/health/charlotte-child-medical-marijuana/.

2. Flowering Hope Foundation home page, last modified 2015, http://www.flowering-hope.co.

Amy Dilullo

VP of Business Development at CMH Brands, Colorado Licensee of Willie's Reserve

"Integrity is everything; staying true to your values and what you believe defines you as a person."

WOMEN AND MEN have been drawn to the cannabis industry for a wide array of reasons: love of the plant, passion for business, deep-seated activism, and, of course, the prospect of making truckloads of money. However, Amy's route didn't follow any of these typical avenues. Born and raised in the Midwest, Amy is a family oriented person with ambitions that, at one time, resembled those of her father's—a physician who owns and operates a number of urgent care clinics in Ohio. Amy felt certain that she possessed her father's "science gene" when she accepted a graduate scholarship in the Clinical Exercise Physiology program at Indiana University. "I was tasked with organizing clinical research studies focused on the health habits of college freshmen while taking classes in chemistry, physiology, and the performance of elite athletes," she recalls. Fairly early on in her graduate studies, Amy realized that the coursework was not inspiring her. "I was concerned that I was investing so much of my time into something I didn't enjoy or see the value in long-term. It wasn't an easy realization, but it got me thinking more about what would bring me joy and fulfillment."

Amy took a long hard look at her life, asking herself what was missing from her world. "It was at this time that I realized I wasn't a particularly spiritual person. I wasn't practicing yoga nor was I devoted to a religion. I decided to begin studying the process of becoming more spiritual." She began learning as much as she could about Eastern religions, particularly Buddhism, but was surprised by how little information was available to her in the Midwest. She eventually discovered a Buddhist center in Colorado that offered a variety of programs where participants could work at the center while learning Buddhist practices and traditions. "I decided to apply for the program, was accepted and offered a role as Lead Chef in the center's kitchen, and that was it! I packed everything up in my car and headed out to Colorado to the Shambhala Mountain Center." Her voice trails off as she adds that her "parents were not exactly thrilled."

While practicing and working at the Center, Amy met a cannabis caregiver and cultivator from the Denver area. "This was 2008, a time when people could grow cannabis pretty much anywhere and then sell it to medical cannabis centers around the state," she remembers. "He and

I built a relationship during my time at Shambhala and, as the program came to a close, he offered me a job helping him in his cannabis business. So there I was, jumping from one very unique environment at this Buddhist Center to another very unique environment within a cannabis cultivation facility."

Despite her parent's concerns and objections, Amy was an avid cannabis user from the age of 15. "I had used cannabis both medically and recreationally. Medically, cannabis helped me cope with stress, anxiety, depression, and [insomnia]. Recreationally, cannabis enhanced fun experiences I would share with my friends." Her parents' concerns returned in full force when Amy disclosed her new career plan: leaving the Buddhist Center and working for a grow operation. Amy is a second generation Italian American and conservative values rule her "large Italian family." Amy's father, the physician, was always against her cannabis use. "He could not understand my devotion to this plant or industry since cannabis was not only federally illegal but also illegal at the state level." This concern existed throughout the first five or six years of Amy's career only ending after what Amy refers to as the "Sanjay Gupta effect."

After Dr. Sanjay Gupta and other medical professionals changed their once anti-marijuana stances and became supporters of medical marijuana, Amy believes that other professionals in the medical field started to become more curious. Her father began his own search for science-based evidence, leading him to research that ultimately convinced him that cannabinoids had true pharmacological benefit. "I think my father saw a medical professional [Dr. Sanjay Gupta], with a voice based in science, approving use of cannabis for medicine, and it helped change his opinion and his receptivity to the plant. This was a discernible gift to our family." Her family may not have changed their minds overnight, but are now incredibly supportive of Amy and her work in the industry. Her parents have toured cultivation facilities alongside Amy, her cousins have come out to visit dispensaries, and everyone in the family talks about her work openly. "What I love most is hearing my father and family educating others. They are changing conversations in their own communities."

Amy's friends, those from her past and those she has met through the industry, have always been supportive. "My friends from high school all know I have been using cannabis for a long time so no one was surprised." She laughs and adds, "Most of my long-term friends feel this was the most relevant career path among all of our peers."

As Amy worked for the caregiver in Denver for six to eight months, she assisted with day-to-day operations and provided sales support. She remembers driving around the state with pounds of weed and bags of cash in her car. "That's how things were back then—the Wild Wild West!"

When Colorado House Bill 1284 was passed in 2010, the landscape of the cannabis business changed entirely. The new bill outlawed the existing caregiver model, requiring all growers to be licensed by the state. "I remember seeing this happen and I realized I needed to shift quickly into a licensed facility. I transitioned into dispensary management and operations," Amy rose quickly within the industry and soon became the Director of Operations, Marketing, and Compliance for a licensed medical dispensary in central Denver. "I invested an enormous amount of time and learned a lot, but I started to see that there wasn't a lot of vertical growth opportunity for me." The competition was fierce as the medical market became more robust and continued to expand. At that time, Amy was approached to work for *KUSH Magazine* in a sales support role, but, after just two days on the job, was promoted to run the entire magazine as the Director of Sales and Marketing.

It was such a rollercoaster! This is where I really learned how to sell from some master saleswomen. Beyond that, I learned how to be a more artful and flexible negotiator who could understand the person I was directing the sale towards and adapt. I was there for a little over a year and then the publishing world shifted, the cannabis industry shifted, and it was time to move forward.

At this time, Amy began building and managing a portfolio of cannabis and non-cannabis clients for whom she would consult on sales and marketing. "But the cannabis industry kept calling me back. Out of a natural evolution of one of these relationships, I was offered a full-time job as the Director of Sales for an early stage CO2 extraction company during a time when CO2 cannabis oil was not cool and not well received. I had to build demand for a product people didn't know they wanted."

Amy is referring to a time in the cannabis industry where most extract connoisseurs preferred BHO (Butane Hash Oil) extracted products over CO2 extracted products.

> I had to educate *and* pitch companies on the benefits of CO2 at the same time. It was hard, but I did it. I was able to grow [the company's] retail distribution and revenue channels dramatically month-over-month. I felt impactful and powerful. I was able to drive major change in a short amount of time. I established a following for their brand and niche product in just 12 months before returning to my own consulting work.

Amy went on to work with some of Colorado's leading marijuana-infused product manufacturers, providing business development support and high-level consulting. A lot of hard work—and some serious heartache—led Amy to her current role as the VP of Business Development for CMH brands, the Colorado licensee for Willie's Reserve, a nationally recognized cannabis brand built around Willie Nelson and his love for cannabis.

> I went through a time when a collision of personal and professional relationships left me questioning not only my goals but my sense of self. It was the hardest and most spiritually challenging time of my life. It took me to the border of everything: the border of emotional strength, the border of mental strength, the border of identity. I eventually had to make a hard decision. I remember taking a step back from all of the noise so I could have a moment of clarity. I saw the industry as a whole

and I knew there would be more and better opportunities for me. It was a big jump, I had nothing lined up, but I knew I had to do it. It was terrifying, utterly terrifying—and it turned out to be one of the most empowering and defining experiences of my life.

And jump, she did. Without a net. But, because of that jump, she wound up (literally) sitting at a table at which she may never have otherwise had a seat.

Almost three months later, I was at the Women Grow Leadership Summit listening to a panel presented by a dear friend of mine, Genifer Murray. After the panel, Genifer took me aside and pointed to two women and said, "You need to go talk to them." Sure enough, across from us were Annie Nelson, Willie Nelson's wife, and Elizabeth Garret Hogan, the VP of Brand for Willie's Reserve. With no preparation for this moment, I gave them the Amy Dilullo Elevator Pitch. They understood me, what I brought to the table, and what I was passionate about—and it aligned with their goals and what they were looking for. I never would have been at that table or in this position if I hadn't taken that risk and that leap.

Amy finds it fascinating that, with a little bit of grit and determination, some of our darkest times can lead us into new heights.

I remember, a year ago, being invited to Austin, Texas, to spend time at Willie's ranch. I was enjoying a fantastic celebrity chef curated dinner that was supporting one of Willie's charities. The band Green River Ordinance was playing and I had just smoked a joint—with Willie Nelson. The moment was pure joy. Pure joy. And I realized that none of this would have been possible without the risk.

Working for CMH Brands as the VP of Business Development is absolutely Amy's "dream job." The product line features a wide selection and promises high quality strains and consistency. A clear picture of the brand is painted on williesreserve.com: "It's as if the Red Headed Stranger has offered an invitation aboard the Honeysuckle Rose to sample the choicest selections of his stash." Amy says she is currently focused on "accelerating business development, growing sales distribution and revenue, developing channel marketing programming, brand strategy, and aligning consumer segmentation with new product development in and outside of the cannabis space." While timing and chance had a lot to do with Amy getting an opportunity to pitch to Willie's Reserve, her tenacity, fearlessness, and ability to deliver earned her the job.

According to Amy, persistence and being comfortable taking risks are a huge part of finding success in the cannabis industry. "You're going to have a lot of setbacks, but you have to keep moving forward. It's a very trying industry, so many people stop grinding it out and don't make it." Amy leans heavily on a close-knit group of friends and colleagues, as well as her family, for support. "My best friend, Genifer Murray, has been my guiding light in the storm. Without her, I wouldn't be here. She's the friend that has no problem telling me to get my act together! You need a cheerleader and someone who helps you to pull yourself up by your britches."

Buoyed by the support she receives from her strong friendships and family ties, Amy sets out to lead and works to emulate other strong female leaders, both within and outside the world of cannabis. Within the industry, Amy has found herself modeling after AC Braddock, CEO of Eden Labs. She describes AC as an incredibly well-spoken, well positioned, and impactful leader. "There is something about her energy and presence, and the way she carries herself, that makes me want to follow in her footsteps." Perpetually well rounded, Amy also looks for inspiration outside of her industry and has found it by reading about CoCo Chanel's story—growing up as the daughter of a seamstress, finding her passion for fashion, and building a world-renowned brand. Michelle Obama has also moved Amy substantially during her time as First Lady. "I am so impressed and in awe of her. She is a leader and a mentor for so many generations, and I think the fact that so many people are saddened, even brought to tears, by the thought of her exiting the White House speaks volumes about the impact she was able to have. I can only hope to carry myself with as much class as she has."

Following the lead of women like AC, CoCo Chanel and Michelle Obama has helped Amy to cope better with the disadvantages that sometimes come with being a woman in business. "There have been many situations where being a woman has helped me, whether it's by relating better with clients or customers or helping people to be more comfortable [in conversations surrounding cannabis] . . . but there have been times where it is a huge disadvantage, too."

Amy recalls moments where she has felt like a sexual object and where she did not seem to be taken seriously by male professionals. "I felt more like a target," she states matter-of-factly. As the industry continues to change and an influx of white collar professionals find their way into the space, Amy feels women need to have a fresh, stronger approach to interacting with these new associates within their business structures.

[Women] need to maintain the strength of our connections. We need to stay focused on the big picture, instead of becoming distracted by conflict between groups and individuals. My favorite analogy is this: our industry is like a large Italian family. When you go to a family dinner with 30 Italians, everyone has something to gripe about. Maybe your Aunt Maria is still bitter because Aunt Stella forgot to bring the right prosciutto last time; or maybe Uncle Martino had to fire Uncle Vito's friend and they don't want to speak to each other right now—but they all sit down at the table together. Because you're family.

Similarly, we need to bind together as an industry. At the end of the day, we're still a family, and we still need to show up at the table. Not doing so holds us all back. We have to remember our goals are shared and we need to realize we are up against greater, unknown forces. Maybe it's Big Pharma, maybe it's Big Tobacco, maybe it's Big Money, maybe it's the new administration. We don't yet know what we are going to battle the most in the years ahead, but we do know we have an opportunity to build Big Canna—and *we can only do it if we get back on the same page and power through this together.*

Amy is confident that women can drive this effort better than anyone, finding and solidifying common ground between business owners, activists, the industry's newcomers, and its pioneers. And, whether or not she realizes it, Amy is an extremely important piece of this puzzle. Beyond her persistence and "won't accept no for an answer" attitude, Amy is very highly regarded and admired. She's often more quiet about her opinions than others are, leading by example instead. "I work really hard and I don't make a lot noise," she laughs, bringing to light that she is truly humble and gracious about her many successes.

Amy ranks integrity at the top of her list of important traits a person within the cannabis industry should possess, and she absolutely "walks the walk."

> Integrity is everything; staying true to your values and what you believe defines you as a person. At the end of the day, this is what's most important: you have to be able to sleep with yourself at night. If you get into a situation where an entity or person or policy is asking you to compromise your integrity, then you should remove yourself—I can't emphasize this enough. The way you hold yourself and the integrity you have is essential. Other people see it and it can inspire people to maintain their own strength and values.

Years ago, Amy and her former dispensary team were part of the Amendment 64 Task Force, the group charged with helping to draft and revise cannabis legislation in Colorado. She remembers a sign that hung on the door through which they entered each meeting: Integrity means doing the right thing even when no one is watching.

Amy Dilullo takes this mantra to heart each and every day, staying true to her word and never cutting corners. She deserves the bright future that undoubtedly lies ahead of her, one which she hopes will include national and international cannabis business development. She has an "undying passion" for traveling and exploring untapped markets, specifically the process of figuring out what product or strategy will work best in a new market or with a new brand. While Amy jokes that someday she'll open a tropical beachside dispensary, she acknowledges that the best things often come to you without a plan. "It's about relationships, curiosity, and being open-minded—and it will be interesting to see which doors open for me and my peers in this industry in the future."

Meg Sanders

CEO OF MINDFUL

"Having a partner who understands what it takes, who isn't intimidated by what you do and who you are is so important.
I'm lucky to have found that."

Anyone who has spent time researching women in cannabis—or the cannabis industry in general—is likely to have come across Megan Sanders. Since 2009, Meg has been serving as a figurehead for her company, MiNDFUL, as well as the industry at large. And many would agree that she is perfect for the role. This well-spoken single mother and cannabis industry pioneer has been featured on a range of media outlets, from local programming to national outlets like *60 Minutes*, and has consistently put her face, and left her mark, on the industry. Like many women in the industry, Meg's partners and colleagues recognized the benefit of having a woman represent MiNDFUL; women make many of the household decisions relating to medicine and healthcare and mothers have, for generations, been the primary caregivers for their children and families. Identifying a woman, like Meg, who is willing to speak to the industry, to its naysayers, and even to those who stand in staunch opposition to her work has made a hugely positive difference for the MiNDFUL brand.

But Meg is much more than a figurehead. As the CEO of MiNDFUL, a Colorado-based company with medical and recreational dispensaries, a sizable 40 thousand square foot cultivation facility, and state-of-the-art extraction capabilities, Meg has been involved in all corners of the industry. Beyond working with her colleagues to develop and build out MiNDFUL, Meg has been extremely influential in Colorado, as well as other states looking for guidance on how to best develop rules and regulations, most notably New York; Connecticut; Massachusetts; Nevada; California; and, most recently, Tennessee. Meg has been sought out by a wide range of clientele, state regulators as well as lobbyists and private investment companies, to help guide various groups and initiatives. But her reputation, and this work, didn't fall into her lap easily.

"Before cannabis, I was working for a family-run office that focused on investment strategy. I worked with about 20 guys ensuring that operating agreements were drafted correctly while also managing the company's compliance department," she recalls, "experience that ultimately translated well into cannabis." Simultaneously, Meg's husband, who she has since divorced, found out that his brother was diagnosed with cancer. In severe pain, he was being treated with serious doses of morphine and Meg remembers vividly the first time she and her husband talked about getting him cannabis to treat his worsening pain. "This was the first time I started thinking about cannabis as a medicine. [His brother] was on morphine and sleeping close to 20 hours per day. With cannabis, he was able to sit at the table, spend time with his family, eat, and be far more comfortable. This experience really started to shift my thinking [about cannabis]." While her experience with her brother-in-law certainly brought cannabis onto her radar, Meg hadn't considered getting into the business herself. At least, not until she heard a family friend was going to create a cultivation facility just outside of downtown Denver.

The conversation to officially get into cannabis kicked off in 2009. Meg remembers thinking, "The horses were leaving the stable! I had never thought of it as an industry before, but I pushed [this friend] and convinced him to let me help with the project." Shortly thereafter, the rules and regulations were released and Meg sat down for a formal interview. The role would involve a heavy amount of paperwork and compliance oversight, something Meg knew well from her work with the investment firm, and she was hired on the spot. "I wasn't being paid immediately. I was doing two jobs and then finally I took the leap, stopped working for the trading company, and came into cannabis full-time." She pauses as she speaks, and then laughs, "I remember the first time I walked into the grow! I thought to myself, *Oh my God, I'm going to prison!*" The company began developing other positions, hiring, and building out business plans, and when its first CEO was terminated for cause, the discussion about finding a replacement arose. "We were fortunate to have a corporate coach working with us at this time to help guide us through this very new industry and its processes. I will never forget sitting down as a team with our coach and hearing him say to the group, 'You guys don't need to find a CEO. She is sitting right here.'" The team agreed and soon after Meg was promoted to role of CEO. She has poured her heart and soul into MiNDFUL, which has risen to national recognition, existing in both Colorado and Illinois with brand expansion plans in the works.

Entering the cannabis industry isn't the only big decision Meg has had to make. She also had to decide whether or not to tell her family about the nature of her new venture, as she was unsure how they would respond. "I still remember telling my family. [The response from] my son, Alijah, who was 18 at the time, stays with me: 'If there's anyone that is going to do this, it's my mom!' I didn't come clean with my [own] mom or my extended family for some time." Alijah joined his mother at MiNDFUL after graduating from college and has since moved on to develop his own successful extraction company.

Meg is an open book when it comes to the challenges she faced working within a male dominated industry – and she has some scars to prove it. "This industry and work has been incredibly, incredibly hard," she reflects, "the battle isn't over when you get through the ceiling. . . . Even if cannabis is more supportive of women than in other industries, which I do believe to be true, no industry operates in a vacuum. Women will still be engaged with men on the technology side, the legal side and the investment side, and there they will, once again, most likely, be sitting at a table amongst a bunch of white men."

Working alongside men wasn't new to Meg. The trading world is male dominated and Meg remembers believing that "this was just how things were. I thought you just had to buck up and deal with it. To be the most effective as a female in these spaces, you need to learn how to be heard. It's not a skill you're born with. I felt, initially, that I really had to stomp my feet or slam my fists on the table just to have a voice."

As her role at MiNDFUL began to take shape and the workload began to exceed what most would consider normal working hours, Meg began running into problems at home. For years prior to entering cannabis, Meg was the consummate working mother, gracefully navigating her professional work without ever dropping the ball at home caring for her children, husband, and household. Cannabis began to change this, requiring Meg to work longer hours and to travel away from home for great lengths of time. The shift in Meg's routine meant she needed support from her husband in new ways, and this caused tension in their relationship. She confides,

I remember the day my marriage ended in my head! I was running around the state and asked my husband of 17 years if he could pick up the dry cleaning. The switch was so big! He replied angrily, and without hesitation, "*I am not your assistant.*" I was done. I had spent years doing both, but realized in that moment, after many years of arguing about my career and ambitions, that my ex could not handle that I was going to be a leader in this company and would need his support at home.

Rising up in MiNDFUL was simply the "straw that broke the camel's back," but she admits that "the problems were there all along."

Leaving her husband and ending their marriage was, undoubtedly, another difficult decision for Meg, and not simply from an emotional perspective. Exiting her marriage meant that many of the childcare and household responsibilities she had attempted to split with her partner rested, once again, squarely on her shoulders. Meg was a newly-single mother of two with a son in college and a daughter who was in elementary school. Being available for her two children has always been of the utmost importance to Meg, and while she felt MiNDFUL understood and respected this, she remembers feeling that her team (of primarily men) couldn't possibly understand the stress that accompanies being thrust into the role of a single mother *and* CEO at the same time. "All of them have incredibly supportive wives at home raising and caring for their children while they work." At this time, MiNDFUL was in the midst of fundraising and Meg recalls many of the "big decisions and big conversations" happening outside of normal business hours. "Business deals and discussions are notorious for happening after hours, after 5:30 p.m. If you're a woman and don't have a strong partner at home, you can't be there and you might fail. I didn't have that luxury at home." Meg worked closely with her founding partners to find balance as best as she could.

Even in a conversation focused on the subject of professional growth and burgeoning industry, it becomes clear that personal relationships are an important part of this equation. As Meg pointed out, "no industry operates in a vacuum," which means that breaking the grass ceiling cannot happen in a vacuum, either. Without support from loved ones or a strong partner, the ceiling can feel impossibly out of reach. Meg's candor and emotions were laid bare as she shared that she has recently "found [her] person because of cannabis. Having a partner that isn't intimidated or threatened, is so important. If you don't have that, it is so incredibly hard to be a leader. I am the luckiest woman. Sheryl Sandberg[1] said it best: you have to pick the right partner to support your goal."

Beyond finding a supportive partner, Meg feels strongly that women must recognize that men should not be broadly generalized as unsupportive of female empowerment and success. There are many men, in and outside of cannabis, eager to support women in their journey to the top of this industry. Her commentary here is valuable as the battle to break through the ceiling is not one women can, or should, take on alone. She shares that everyone is responsible for seeking equality in this industry, for women as well as minorities. Stereotyping men alienates those who are fighting in the trenches alongside the progressive women in cannabis. "What hurts [my partner] the most, is when he hears me talking about the role white men have in women not climbing the ranks. I've realized it's incredibly hard for him to deal with that. He reminds me sometimes not to lump him in."

As MiNDFUL began to flourish, it became more and more evident that Meg, in her role as a figurehead, had the power to shift the thinking of others, influence change, and draw a new customer base to the stores and to the industry. "My partners really saw the value in [me] putting my face out there in the public—and the risk, especially as a single mother, was massive! I truly believed that, because of my work branding us and helping to rebrand the industry, I would have more of a voice at the table when it came to business decisions, but that wasn't entirely the case." Meg divulges that there were occasions when she felt "drowned out" by her male counterparts, and cautions; "Until we hold [men] accountable, it's never going to change." Meg also points out that, as the leader of a company, she is often the person to receive accolades and recognition, whether in the media or among her colleagues, but, conversely, she is also the one to bear the blame when things go wrong. "If anything happens with the company that is headline worthy, good or bad, it's not MiNDFUL, it's Meg Sanders."

To witness firsthand the incredible burden Meg bears, one needs to look no further than watching her answer Bill Whitaker's intense interview questions during a 2015 episode of *60 Minutes*[2]. Meg's ability to handle herself in this high-pressure situation with extraordinary poise demonstrates that she is well versed in acting with equanimity as the face of MiNDFUL and an ambassador of the cannabis industry as a whole. It's a role few women have chosen for themselves, and with good reason. Meg has been scrutinized by fellow professionals, activists, the media, and even other parents and families who do not understand or agree with her work. It's also a role that does not end at five o'clock, or on weekends, or while traveling. Meg is recognizable and pursued—almost constantly—by people who want her opinion and her attention. She has to keep sharp at all times, something that would take a toll on anyone, but especially a woman juggling her business, the industry's efforts, and motherhood.

While honest about her concerns and frustrations, Meg is also reflective about the many things she has learned, especially as those lessons relate to her communication style, specifically in meetings. "One thing women seem to spend much more time thinking about, than men do, in board room environments is how to be the most effective communicator so that you are heard and that things get done. I realized, over time, that my delivery wasn't always perfect and that I had to make a lot of changes to be more effective as a leader among a team of men." Her candor is refreshing as is her thoughtful advice for men who may be "unaccustomed to having women drive the conversation. . . . Some men have been socialized to believe that the world will adapt to them. But no. They need to be adapting and evolving, too!" She emphasizes that both women *and* men need to work hard at evolving, and if a woman realizes that the people around her are not willing to adapt and evolve, it's important for her to accept that she may not be able to change their minds or fix the problem. While the advice to walk away from those who cannot seem to change their thinking may seem defeatist, the reality is that there are many men who are genuinely interested in working alongside strong women and, as Meg expresses, it can be wiser to seek out those partners and forge ahead with their support.

Meg is very aware of the fact that her struggle is similar to the struggles of many other women throughout the industry, but also notes that she feels a powerful shift happening. "Women are slowly, but surely, becoming a force." She is a huge proponent of women entering this market and believes they should "get in it right now! There is so much need in this industry . . . if you have an idea that you think can translate into cannabis, get involved!" She cautions that "breaking up with a financial partner is harder than breaking up a marriage," so choosing business partners needs to be a well-researched decision. Meg emphasizes a point brought up by almost every successful woman in cannabis, expressing that women entering this industry should hire an attorney to protect their own personal interests, not simply to protect their company at large. "Make sure everything is documented properly. Read the documents, hire someone you can trust to help you interpret the documents—this paperwork is what will protect you in the end, so get everything in writing."

To conclude her words of advice, Meg stresses that it is important for female entrepreneurs to have other women in their corner who understand their intentions and long-term goals.

Jaime Lewis has been my biggest life ring. Having her in my presence—she's my sunshine on the beach. If I'm having a moment, I can turn to Jaime Lewis or Genifer Murray, two fellow CEOs and friends in the cannabis space. These two women have been so invaluable to me during this journey and we have so much mutual respect for one another. When I look around and see many of the women who have been on this road with me for the past six years, I immediately respect them more because they're still here. And if you're still here, that tells me something important about who you are.

In the cannabis industry, time is often likened to dog years, and Meg clearly understands that anyone who has been able to navigate this tumultuous landscape over a long period of time deserves great respect.

Of all her triumphs, Meg is without hesitation as she shares that the best part of her experience in cannabis has been the people with whom she works. "If I never made another dollar in this space, it wouldn't matter, because you can't put a value on these relationships. These people have become a part of who I am and I am so grateful to count these human beings as my blessings along what has been a hard journey." As she looks toward the future, Meg Sanders is optimistic about the work she has before her. "I am going to capitalize on the value that I bring to the table in a way that makes me happy. I plan to keep fighting for equality in the workplace, but have also decided to spend more time listening to my heart and soul. Life is too short not to—and yes, cannabis taught me that."

Notes

1. Sheryl Sandberg, *Lean In: Women, Work, and the Will To Lead* (New York: Alfred A. Knopf, 2013).

2. Bill Whitaker, "Colorado Pot," *60 Minutes*, season 47, episode 17, produced by Marc Lieberman, aired January 11, 2015 (CBS), http://www.cbsnews.com/news/colorado-pot-marijuana-60-minutes/.

Amy Poinsett and Jessica Billingsley

CO-FOUNDERS OF MJ FREEWAY

"Our greatest assets walk out of the door every night—we have worked so hard to build this team and to develop this culture; our people are the heart and soul of the company."

SEVEN YEARS AGO, the high tech industry had its horizons expanded enormously when Jessica Billingsley (COO) and Amy Poinsett (CEO) teamed up to found MJ Freeway, one of the cannabis industry's leading technology companies. Beyond building a business that has permanently altered the cannabis landscape, Jess and Amy developed a company with a strong corporate culture that has, since day one, been one of the industry's strongest supporters of women.

Before joining the cannabis industry, Amy and Jess each owned technology companies. Jess remembers the day, back in 2009, when she was first asked about investing in a dispensary. "I remember when, after I invested, a team member asked that I recommend software that they should implement in the store. That's when I first saw our opportunity," recalls Jess, "so I approached Amy who, very famously, said, 'One hundred percent yes! Let's do that!' and we started having conversations about what we could build and launch in this space."

It didn't take long for both women to agree that this was, indeed, a superb opportunity, the kind that doesn't appear very often, so they worked swiftly to finalize their business structure. Jess removed herself as one of the dispensary's investors and owners to prevent any conflict of interest, and Amy and Jess launched their company, MJ Freeway. The two remember the early days vividly; it was a time when resources were constrained. "It wasn't like it is today. It was extremely difficult to raise money and it was also hard to attract top talent to an industry existing in such a grey market," Jess remembers.

Before starting the recruitment process, Amy and Jess sought legal counsel to assess risk. When they got the green light from legal, they felt ready to look for team members. Amy remembers sharing the lawyer's feedback with prospective candidates to try to prove to them that the risks were minimal, but many people were still turning down positions. "It was certainly different from today where we get cold calls every single day from people wanting to work with us. Back then, it was probably close to 50% of the people we wanted to hire said no." Interestingly enough, through their struggle to attract top talent, Jess and Amy began to recognize that there was a particular demographic they could potentially incentivize to join the company in a unique way: women.

> We knew there were a lot of female developers disenfranchised with the technology industry; many of them were starting families and had established careers, but had limited room to rise within technology. We decided if we could offer them a more flexible schedule, working 25 to 30 hours per week exclusively for us, that we might be able to draw women into the business. The idea worked and, over time, part of our company's story most definitely became "women helping women."

MJ Freeway continues to offer a working environment supportive of women. Amy and Jess don't hesitate for a second when answering the question: What is the most important asset to your company? "Our greatest assets walk out of the door every night—we have worked so hard to build this team and to develop this culture; our people are the heart and soul of the company." Both Amy and Jess feel fortunate for the women who took a risk by joining them early on. They knew all too well how hard that decision could be for a female, especially if she did not have support from her family. Neither Amy nor Jess felt that they could rely on their own families for support of any kind, especially funding. Jess shares, "Neither of our families were supportive of this idea, so it is a good thing that we didn't need a ton of their support early on. My parents have come around, but in the early days it was very embarrassing for them." Amy's experience with her parents, who she describes as "older and very conservative," closely mirrors Jessica's. Amy adds, "I don't believe my parent's friends have any idea what I do. I think my parents are happy for me now, but still uncomfortable sometimes. I honestly wonder how my parents talk about me!" She laughs, adding, "And now my sister has joined MJ Freeway, so my parents can't discuss what either of their daughters do!"

In 2010, Jess and Amy officially incorporated the business and began developing the product. They funded the business entirely out of pocket, not taking salaries of any kind for the first two years. The duo remembers the process of finding capital being an incredible challenge, forcing them to self-fund. Jess describes this volatile time:

> We bet everything on this. In 2011, we were not successful in rais-ing funding of any kind—even though we had a track record! In 2010, the year we incorporated, we sold at least one license per day for the first three months—unheard of growth—but it wasn't enough. Funding was so hard to come by. There were a lot of raids and people were scared. I remember going back to investors in 2012, who had said no to equity investments, to talk with them about obtaining bridge loans. It was actually in 2012 when we flipped into profitability, but we were teetering there. We had al-ready spent the bridge loans and now election season was upon us. [The 2012 election] was the most terrifying time for us as a busi-ness. Fortunately, we had a stellar outcome from that election and, within two months, we had paid back every single bridge loan.

The company grew rapidly from a small team of 12 people in 2013 to 71 people at the time of publishing, and has been first to market with ev-ery single software feature they have offered. In 2016, they successfully closed their Series C round of funding—raising eight million dollars and were the second company to get true, mainstream venture capital funding into the cannabis sector. The investment was used to continue scaling their team and developing their next generation of products. "It has been so exciting," Jess shares, "I am so pleased to see how well the product has been received. I couldn't sleep the night before the round—I felt like a kid before Christmas!" While the company grows substantially, Amy and Jess remain committed to their employees by continuing to offer an incredibly competitive benefits package and by hosting a Monday morning company-wide discussion during which any employee can tune into the webinar to share ideas and hear about the company's strategic goals.

Jess and Amy have navigated the cannabis industry, as well as the investment and technology industries, with grace and with class. When asked if the cannabis industry is more or less welcoming to women than other industries, like high tech, both Amy and Jess had a lot to share. Jess expresses,

> There are obviously pros and cons to everything and there are disadvantages that women face in technology as well as in cannabis. You will always be remembered when you are the only woman in the room and there are advantages that come with that, too. I think, overall, it's easier for women in cannabis. Yes—it's been very male dominated, but I think it's easier, in part, because of our counter-culture. There is a quality of acceptance of people, not just women, but all people. That said, it is still very tough for women.

Amy shares much of Jess' sentiment, but also adds that we, as an industry, are not doing women any favors by presenting the industry as "easier for women," saying,

> While we want to support women getting involved; I don't think we are helping women by giving them rose-colored glasses. The reality is that this is a very tough business, and I believe it is tougher women than it is for men. It's important for women to realize that they will still be the minority, especially when they go to raise funding, as an example, as they are heading into a one hundred percent male dominated world. Being a good business owner is much, much harder in this industry—especially being in a [federally] illegal, super competitive sector. . . . The deck is stacked against you, and women need to be ready to face that.

Jess continues, stating, "Let's be clear. When [the industry] started there were almost no women in cannabis. I believe if you compared the numbers—women in cannabis versus women in other industries—there would be far less women in cannabis than is reported . . . I think some of what is being reported is a fabrication of numbers." Their honest take is not meant to be discouraging. The two feel strongly that this *is* a great industry for women to join, but they should do so without any misconceptions as this industry is extremely difficult—a serious reality that Amy and Jess faced in January 2017.

In November 2016, MJ Freeway launched MJ Platform, the cannabis industry's brand new enterprise software platform which serves to acknowledge that cannabis *needs* next generation technology, consulting, data, and more. The product was designed to bring together each of these needs in one comprehensive solution. The company's highly anticipated and successful launch at the MJ Business Daily Conference in Las Vegas involved the development of an interactive experience called Immerse. Immerse was a beautifully designed "dispensary of the future" allowing conference-goers to move through the mock dispensary while interacting with various technologies, some belonging to MJ Freeway and some belonging to partner technology companies. The launch was a huge success and MJ Freeway entered 2017 as the dominating player in the cannabis technology space. "Being able to bring technology, data, and consulting together and offer a tailored and comprehensive solution" was a high point, Jess expresses, adding, "This is where our company is laser-focused; we want to be in every market, including international markets."

Unfortunately, the launch took a turn for the worst in January 2017 when the company fell victim to "an unprecedented, malicious attack," words used by MJ Freeway in their response to the incident. The company issued a statement on January 14, 2017 by uploading a video to YouTube featuring Amy speaking about the attack as well as their efforts to get companies back online, securely. She announced,

> On Sunday morning, attackers took down both MJ Freeway's production and backup servers, causing an outage for all of our clients. I am incredibly sorry for the impact this has had on your businesses. Keeping our clients' data secure has always been a top priority.

Current analysis shows that the attackers did not extract any client or patient data, and did not view any patient data thanks to encryption measures we had in place. This attack impacted you, your patients, and the entire industry. We are channeling our outrage into action. Since Monday, we have been working to get hundreds of clients online with alternate MJ Freeway sites. Setting up these sites involves calling clients, one by one, and staying on the phone with them until their site is live. [This process] is taking more time than we'd like it to, but we are doing whatever it takes to get clients back on their feet and secure. This outage is a unique situation, *caused by an unprecedented, malicious attack*. The damage from the attack is extensive, but much is repairable. In response to this attack, all client sites have been migrated to a new, more secure environment. It's one of many measures we are taking to bolster our defenses. Our team is working around the clock for you. You mean everything to us. And we are committed to serving you today, tomorrow, and into the future. Thank you for your continuing support.

The attack is believed to be the first of its kind in cannabis, and will test the strength of Amy, Jess, and their entire team of employees. Fortunately for MJ Freeway, the company has two of the most powerful, strong and relentless women at its helm who will stop at nothing to repair the damage, rectify all concerns with their clients, and push forward. This is most certainly the darkest and most challenging time in their company's history, but, as they have done in the past, these women will rebound and rise above the misfortune. Amy Poinsett and Jessica Billingsley built MJ Freeway on a strong foundation of corporate culture where they have supported women and men alike and garnered unwavering loyalty along the way. Now more than ever, the two will rely on their human assets as they surmount this obstacle, get back on track, and continue growing nationally.

Julie Dooley

PRESIDENT OF JULIE'S NATURAL EDIBLES

"Finding people to share this journey with, who truly know the trials and tribulations I am dealing with, has been the most important decision I have made in this process."

MANY PEOPLE HAVE fond childhood memories of their mothers or grand-mothers baking for them—the smells, the warmth of the oven, and the feeling that these foods were truly made with love. This nostalgia brings them back to times in their lives when they felt cared for and nourished by people who loved them unconditionally. Capturing this essence in a brand is difficult because this feeling is extremely hard to replicate in a food manufacturing facility. But it is part of what makes Julie Dooley and her business, Julie's Natural Edibles, so wonderfully unique. By setting out to make edibles that are both delicious and healthy, she has successfully found a way to create products that people can enjoy while also feeling cared for. As she shares her story, one can't help but wish they were a fly on the wall—or a friend sitting next to her in the kitchen—as she and her co-creator, Kate, began navigating the process of making edibles that are not only good for the body, but also good for the soul.

Julie's world before cannabis deserves attention because her story is very relatable to many women who may be considering a transition into this business, specifically those who are second guessing their backgrounds and qualifications. Julie holds a degree in genetics from the University of California, a degree she laughs about, saying she "only used the degree to have babies of [her] own!" At school, she met the love of her life, Terry, and, immediately following their graduation in 1993, the two were married. "It wasn't long after our wedding that Terry asked me to move to Denver. I thought, 'What do I care? I'm 24. Sure, let's go to Denver!'" And off they went. Upon their arrival in Colorado, Julie spent some time looking for work in genetics, but quickly learned that, for most professional roles, she would need to have a secondary degree in the field. Instead of going back to school, she took on an assortment of odd jobs—none relating to her degree, but several associated with a lifelong passion she had for finance. "As a little girl, I remember pretending I was a trader. My dad was a stockbroker and used to teach me, and I think it's part of why I was ultimately drawn to genetics—the two fields are both numbers oriented with lots of math and ratios, which I really loved." As Julie navigated her way around Colorado, taking on part-time work and getting to know her new state, she and her husband got pregnant. Julie's warm tone as she recalls this time in her life suggests that she absolutely loved being a stay-at-home mom for her three kids.

As her children reached school age, Julie began engaging with their schools by becoming involved with various boards. It was around this time that Julie saw an advertisement for an open role as a Finance Manager at the University of Denver's preschool. A former board treasurer, Julie applied and was immediately hired. The workload was perfect for her, allowing Julie to maintain balance between motherhood and her job. She remembers the exceptional benefits and her hours being reasonable and somewhat flexible. But all of that changed when the chancellor did a round of layoffs in broad strokes, letting go of close to three hundred employees. "I was not laid off, but instead offered a role with far greater responsibility and workload that would have required two to three times the hours than the role I had. I wasn't looking to alter my life in this way so I decided to take a severance package and consider other options."

At the time of her departure, Julie remembers cannabis becoming a more commonly discussed topic of conversation. "You couldn't turn on the TV without hearing about it at least once. Interestingly enough, at this same time I had become very sick and remained sick until around 2004. No one knew what was wrong with me. I looked sickly, lost a lot of weight, and wasn't feeling well at all." Julie saw a number of specialists and was ultimately diagnosed with Celiac Disease. "

When I was diagnosed, I immediately started reading labels and looking at everything in my food. For me, this is when the lid came off of the "secrets of food," and I realized I needed to make major changes for myself, as well as for my family. I never realized that a piece of bread could keep me sick for the rest of my life.

In severe discomfort from her condition, Julie connected with a local marijuana grower and began using cannabis to help ease the pain and in-flammation. She recalls how much cannabis helped her, especially on the accidental occasions when she ingested gluten. "I was a Deadhead growing up," she laughs, "and my brother was always dragging me to [Grateful] Dead shows! I was of that lifestyle, 'free to be you and me,' but had given it up when I married Terry. He was never into that and it was sort of an end of an era for me—*until* I got sick"

Though Terry supported Julie's cannabis use to treat her pain, it was a secret she kept from her children and many of her friends. However, when she learned that her best friend, Kate, was suffering from a brain tumor, Julie felt it was a good time to share that secret with Kate. "Thank God Kate's tumor was benign, but she still had to undergo surgery. I remember, after her surgery, visiting Kate and seeing her table covered in pills. She didn't want to take anything, so I started buying her cannabis. We got into smoking together, but continued to keep this a secret from most everyone else.

Kate was a mother and successful art director for a major magazine. From an outsider's perspective, neither of these women fit the stereotype of the typical cannabis consumers, but they still felt an uncomfortable pressure to keep their choice of medicine hidden from those who might not understand or those who may have cast judgment.

> I remember one day at Kate's when we were leaving to get the kids from school and we both smelled like cannabis. We hadn't smoked in many, many hours, but we could still smell it. Kate started lending me clothes so we could go to the school to grab our kids without the smell. As she was throwing clothes at me to put on I had an epiphany: this is bullshit. Why are we hiding our medicine?

Julie and Kate continued experimenting with cannabis, trying different strains to see which worked best to treat their individual symptoms, but wanted to turn their attention towards a new method of consumption: edibles.

> We started learning about cannabutter by Googling it and then went out and bought a $400 ounce of Purple Hindu Kush—we knew we liked this strain when we smoked it although, at the time,

we didn't know anything about it. She and I whipped up our first batch [of cannabutter] and gave it a try. We had the most extraordinary experience ever—higher than I had ever been, but feeling incredible, and better than I had ever felt, physically.

When the high faded, the two spent time reflecting on the experience. Julie remembers Kate describing it as "sheer magic," and they both brainstormed how to further fine-tune their recipe. "We had found a way to consume our medicine and we learned how to time our consumption so that, by the time our children were home from school, we were no longer high—and no longer reeked!"

The pair began spending more and more time in the kitchen, Julie leveraging her science background as they refined each formulation. Their secret was also becoming harder to keep and, soon, Julie and Kate found themselves sharing their creations with other close female friends. Some women reached out to Julie after trying the edibles to let her know how much the products helped them. "One woman shared that her anxiety was completely gone while another explained that she no longer had any sciatica pains. Our products were working for people and that inspired us to keep going."

Despite having limited information available to them regarding strain varieties and their unique profiles, Julie and Kate decided early on that they wanted each batch of their edibles to be strain specific. "We didn't know why we were doing it at the time—all we knew is that different strains caused different effects in the body. I didn't understand terpene profiles or know what cannabinoids were; but inside, being the scientist that I am, I knew keeping them separate was going to be important." This became even more clear to Julie on the day she consumed edibles made with a strain called White Widow and had the first serious panic attack of her life.

It truly wasn't because I had too much—I had the wrong variety. Conversely, Kate had a great experience eating from the same batch. Over time, I learned that anything more than 80% sativa isn't going to work for me which made a lot of sense given my, and Kate's, very different physiologies.

Julie describes Kate as large and strong, while Julie was always on the smaller side, especially after years of undiagnosed Celiac Disease that, at one point, caused her weight to fall beneath one hundred pounds.

As far as Julie and Kate were concerned, the two had proof of concept that their products could help others and their next step was to decide if they should create a legitimate business out of their hobby.

> It was a no brainer—in 2010, licenses were $1,200 and my husband, given his background in building out commercial kitchens and supermarkets, had the know-how to get us a kitchen setup quickly. We expected finding a leased property to be difficult, but got lucky when we met "Big John" [who is] still my landlord today. *I wasn't afraid.* The timing was perfect—my kids were the right age for me to be away more often, my husband was supportive—and Kate and I decided to go for it and see what would happen. Beyond that, I was very secure with myself and felt that I had reached a place where I truly liked who I was and was confident in my decisions.

With the details coming together, the two drove to the Marijuana Enforcement Division (MED) offices and got themselves and their business licensed, solidifying their decision to move forward at a commercial level. Their husbands immediately got to work building out a basic 800-square-foot commercial kitchen completing the setup in just one weekend. "It all fell into place. I took it as a sign that we were making a good decision. I couldn't wait to get started." Julie & Kate's, a gluten-free marijuana bakery, opened its doors in August 2011.

That same year, the cannabis industry began to develop more rapidly and, with independent laboratories beginning to open, Julie was delighted to have strain information increasingly available to her.

> As someone with a science background, I couldn't *wait* to have that information. I remember when Genifer Murray of CannLabs first called me. Kate and I had about a $10,000 budget in 2011 and

I swear we spent $9,000 of it on lab testing. I was one of the first people in the industry to say that we desperately needed to know how many milligrams of THC were in these products and I am really proud of that.

It was a dream business for Julie and Kate; they each worked from seven o'clock in the morning to three o'clock in the afternoon so they could continue caring for their children, a luxury that would not have been possible had they also pursued a retail dispensary license or cultivation license. Furthermore, the time they spent with their children even helped them to determine which items to include in their product offering.

> One day, Kate and I were sitting at my table and it occurred to us that our kids didn't really enjoy eating oatmeal or granola—they were gravitating towards chocolates and candies, but didn't like these healthier options. At the same time, Kate and I were trying to figure out how to develop a healthier line of marijuana infused products that women would want to eat and incorporate into their healthy lifestyles. With these two conversations in mind, it occurred to us that we should develop granola and oatmeal based products so children would not want to eat the edibles and women would feel good about eating them.

A lot has changed since 2010, but Julie stays true to her original purpose: to create healthy, gluten-free, infused products of the highest quality. Kate exited the business a few years ago, but the two remain close friends and Julie continues to run the business. As the industry has changed and evolved, so has Julie's role within it:

> I don't think I expected, going into this, how much advocacy work I was going to wind up doing. I remember the first time I went to speak before the President of Denver City Council. It was one of the most challenging things I had done to that point and took

so much courage to open up in front of all of these people who were likely judging me for my work and decision to join the cannabis industry. I've learned that this is part of the industry—putting your face out there—while it has gotten easier over the years, there were still some very trying situations. There is one opposition group in particular that was so hard on me, and the woman who headed up the group had kids at the same school as my kids. I saw her one day at an event to discuss cannabis—we had made eye contact and she was standing with a few other women from the opposition group. I wanted to make things cordial and right so I approached her to talk. Before I could get even a few words out she began yelling at me loudly, "You're feeding your children with drug money! You're an abomination!" I didn't know what to say. It was completely horrible. When I turned around, however, I was met with hugs and care from three younger people also there advocating for the cannabis movement and I realized something that changed me going forward: whatever she said didn't matter. *We're doing the right thing here advocating for this and I am not going to let her drag me down.*

Throughout her years in the business, Julie has endured a number of confrontations like this one; unfortunately, her daughter, Sarah, has, as well. The same woman with whom Julie tried to clear the air at the event, later approached Sarah while she was playing on the school's playground and proceeded to tell Sarah that her mother was not a good person and was selling drugs. Obviously troubled by this woman's behavior, Julie addressed the school's principal and the situation was eventually resolved, but it had shaken her. Since starting Julie and Kate's, Julie has informed her children about marijuana and they are aware of what their mom does for a living. Her daughter, Sarah, is now 16 years old and Julie expresses how incredibly proud she is of her for standing her ground on the playground that day. "I educate my children about this plant. They know it's a medicine that really helps people."

Julie's advocacy and commitment to share her knowledge with others extends well past her own circle of friends and family. Within this movement, she has come to be known as a true ally: a woman who will call meetings with the Marijuana Enforcement Division to influence rule changes, speak out at the city and state levels regarding cannabis legalization, and regularly takes calls from her industry peers to answers question or to offer moral support.

> It's been so empowering having women cheering me on, and I enjoy doing the same. These women—we all understand one another—it is this kind of friendship that saves [me]. The industry is not going to change. It's going to be a brutal workload *every single day*. Finding people to share this journey with, who truly know the trials and tribulations I am dealing with, has been the most important decision I have made in this process.

After facing several extremely difficult challenges in 2016—Julie was sued by a person she trusted; had several massive regulatory changes to deal with, all at an extremely high cost, and was without a formal sales team—she has high hopes for the future.

> I made some strategic hires for sales, spent a substantial amount of time reflecting on what went wrong in 2016, and am looking at identifying partners in other markets. I am bringing in some equity partners to help me scale this business—something I have not done before—but I've realized I need help and want team members to help me fill the gaps. I am thrilled to announce that I have a rockstar CFO joining our team and I believe she will help us tighten up our plans in Colorado before we prepare for national, and even international, opportunities.

Julie also plans to reenergize herself by stepping of the kitchen and back into the field—she loves educating dispensary staff around Colorado about her products; food in general; and food-related allergies and diseases, like Celiac Disease. Additionally, like many other working moms, Julie Dooley will continue striving to balance running her successful company in a developing industry and spending treasured time with her family and friends.

———

Wanda James

CEO OF SIMPLY PURE

"It takes breasts of steel."

"I HAVE BEEN a pothead my entire life." Wanda James is the CEO of Simply Pure, managing partner at the Cannabis Global Initiative (CGI), and anything but apologetic when it comes to discussing her favorite plant: cannabis. As a leading advocate in the industry, she makes her voice heard when it comes to fighting for what she believes in and shaking up the status quo. When Wanda speaks, her passion is palpable. Her enthused tone and colorful, yet deliberate, speech commands attention and respect. For her, being the only woman in a sea of men doesn't phase her: "Don't be afraid. You have to speak up. In a room full of men, you cannot shrink." And Wanda is clearly not one to shrink. She "likes to piss people off" and challenge the system when she knows what she's fighting for is right. Though she's seen other women hesitate before getting into this "crazy industry," it wasn't a difficult choice for her. She and her husband, Scott, were the first Colorado-licensed African Americans to own a dispensary and edible company.

Wanda was the first person in her family to graduate from college. After earning her degree from the University of Colorado in 1986, she was commissioned as an officer in the United States Navy: "the only time I wasn't smoking," she laughs. Her position in Naval Integrated Underwater Surveillance (IUSS) transferred her to Virginia Beach, Bermuda, and New York City. She later graduated from the Los Angeles African American Women's Public Policy Institute at the University of Southern California and is a former President of the National Women's Political Caucus. Wanda was appointed to the L.A. Small and Local Business Commission and sat on the Board of Directors of the Greater Los Angeles African American Chamber of Commerce. At the age of 32, Wanda ran for congress in L.A. Although she lost, her candidacy was very influential and she made many important contacts. From there, she went on to start James Fox Communications. Eventually, Wanda returned to her home state of Colorado to further pursue politics. In 2008, she was appointed to President Obama's National Finance Committee and became one of the largest bundlers of donations in Colorado, raising nearly $250,000 for his campaign.

The idea to enter into cannabis came about in the midst of Wanda's political career. In 1999, her father found out that he had another son, but her father passed away before getting the chance to meet him. This lost opportunity left Wanda with a powerful desire to cultivate a relationship with her sibling. Soon after meeting, she learned that her brother had been serving a 10-year sentence in a Texas federal prison after being busted with four and a half ounces of marijuana—even though he had no violent criminal history. "Up until my brother, I had never known a person who went to jail for pot." Growing up in Colorado, she and her friends came from high income neighborhoods, drove nice cars, and "were all lawyers and doctors and we had all smoked together and it wasn't a big deal." She chuckles and recounts: "We would sit on the steps of Libby Hall and roll joints in preparation for the weekend. If a cop walked by and noticed, he'd ask us to put it away, and we would put it away." That would be that. But after continued conversations with her brother, Wanda started to realize that "the world that I live in is not 'real world America'; I am so *rare*."

Wanda's eyes were opened by her brother's plight: "This was the first time I had seen what poverty means in America. Things that were so simple to us took him three months." Her tone changes when she talks about this. There is a low rumble beneath her words of frustration. Her brother had struggled to find a job as a black man in Texas with a felony record. Because he couldn't get a job, he couldn't afford to register his vehicle or pay his insurance and, therefore, didn't have the use of a car. Not having access to transportation and employment made it virtually impossible for Wanda's brother to be successful; his plight highlighted the way in which minorities can become trapped in the broken system, even with only one non-violent drug conviction. If it was happening to him, it was certainly happening to others. It was hard for Wanda to understand, coming from such a liberal background, so she brought her brother's case to an attorney friend of hers to do a small scale study.

When Wanda's friend sat her down to discuss the findings, Wanda's perspective was completely changed.

It was the first time somebody pulled back the veil for me and showed me that 800,000 people had been arrested for these non-violent crimes. Of that 800,000, nearly 85% were black and brown boys. Because cannabis is so widely used, you can target a group of people because they don't have the means to legally defend themselves. When they aren't able to pay these legal fees, they are thrown into a modern day slave system. *A black boy, my brother, was put in a slave system to pick cotton, literally, to pay for his freedom—this isn't 1965; his whole life was completely fucked.*

After gaining this awareness from her brother's situation and recognizing the importance of the contacts she made during her time in business and politics, Wanda felt it was her distinct responsibility to speak out and fight for what she firmly believes is a social justice issue. She recalls sitting on the porch with her husband saying, "Let's take on cannabis." "We did know it was a good business, but, at the same time, when we did it, we knew that we were going into something that was also a political issue. We had a responsibility to speak out about this." Wanda had the right Rolodex and more than enough business and political experience to dive right into the cannabis industry. At the time, she was not aware that she and her husband were the first African Americans to be licensed. Once she found out, she knew "they weren't going to be able to make the only black people in [the cannabis industry] criminals."

Regardless, Wanda knew she wasn't immune to being harassed or arrested. Almost inevitably, she was raided in 2010 by the Adams County Sheriff's Office. "I was pissed," she says. However, everything that was taken during the raid was returned with a formal apology within 45 minutes, an event Wanda credits "entirely to her political connections." That's because she makes it a point to know everyone. Wanda insists she's not kidding when she says she "has every attorney in the industry on speed dial." She talks to the press, to politicians, to industry attorneys, and countless others. Because of this, she's able to leverage her relationships when she has a problem that needs fixing. She admits that, although she will never break or step over the line of the law, when it comes to fighting for a cause she believes in, she likes to "bend the hell out of the rules." And when it comes to fostering relationships with these people, she emphasizes that "whether you like them or don't like them doesn't matter. *This is business; there's no such thing as permanent enemies or permanent friends.*"

This is powerful advice for aspiring female entrepreneurs in the cannabis industry. Wanda doesn't hesitate to say that "all women need to get into this. A plethora of female growers, business owners, lawyers, designers, extract makers, chefs—and now! By all means, get into this. Especially now—I believe the pressure is off and this is a safe place to do business."

Because cannabis is still federally illegal, it can be a taboo subject, especially when families are involved. Wanda feels she's been able to overcome—or work around—this judgment with the support of her husband and family. However, she still thinks many women are "totally worried about PTA moms" and the like and, therefore, hide their cannabis use. "Some women come into the dispensary every week and their husbands don't even know they buy weed." She thinks it's typically viewed as "a male thing, especially when you look at advertising and the media," But, undoubtedly, Wanda has proven that women *do* have a place and *can* be successful in cannabis. "You've got to understand business, understand your acumen, your hiring practices, marketing—all of it. And you can't break down at work and you can't break down with men. *It takes breasts of steel!*" Wanda laughs, but she understands it's a hardcore industry. Any business hoping to prosper needs to be built with the ability to adapt and grow.

"Here's where we have to be careful. There have been a number of women run out of the businesses *they* started, mind you, by their male investors." She explains:

In 2009, when women started these companies, you had to get money from friends and it's important to be protected against those "friends" of yours that initially invested. Now that these companies are worth something, there are women being pushed out for not being able to "run" their $15 million company. It pisses me off that women "can't handle" a $15 million company. It was all well and fine when they were clearing the path and putting in their blood, sweat, and tears, but, if they didn't work out an ironclad operating agreement, they are in danger. We've got to be careful in holding onto our companies.

That's why Wanda feels it's so necessary to "have warriors on your side. You need these warriors, other women, fighting with you." She describes the "different level of competition" when she's working with other females. "Women really are the village; we understand that, if we each gather enough nuts, we all get to feast. Many men, though, they hoard their nuts for themselves." An amusingly fitting analogy, but, in a serious way, she has experienced how men operate much differently than women in business situations. "I can call up any of my ladies who own dispensaries in the state and be like, 'What the fuck is this?!', and those ladies will come over, help, and spell out for me how to make it work. Even if they are competitors . . . that doesn't happen with men." Wanda can really appreciate and lean on her community of women and attributes a huge factor of her continued success in cannabis to that network of support.

Even with all Wanda has accomplished, she wants to keep building Simply Pure into a "really smart" company. Simply Pure is already credited as the first cannabis edible company in the world to specialize in a healthy alternative to what was initially available on the edibles market. "We were the first to cook with whole bud and the first to guarantee consistent dosing by having a complete staff of professional certified chefs working in a commercial kitchen. The result was creating gourmet products that guaranteed purity and consistency and were 100% organic, vegan, and gluten free"—not to mention delicious! At the 2016 Cannabis Business Awards, Wanda James won the Cannabis Woman of the Year award and Brian Nowak, one of Simply Pure's managers, was selected as Manager of the Year. "Today, Simply Pure has a safe and comfortable location where we are dedicated to creating a positive cannabis experience by providing a sensible alternative to alcohol and prescription drugs." All patrons of the dispensary are honored "as a progressive and courageous force of change."

So what's next for Wanda? "[Simply Pure is] already working internationally. We are working with a number of Caribbean Islands developing their legal structure. For me personally, right now I'm loving being the CEO of Simply Pure, but in the next three to five years, I want to turn the company over to someone with more energy." Wanda's will surely be some big shoes to fill given that she has more energy than most, but for the right "potrepreneur," the opportunity could be there. For Wanda James, her mission is both a personal and political one. Her brother's story may have served as a tipping point, but there is a deeper burning in her heart that keeps her moving forward. "I want to continue fighting for social justice. [The War on Drugs] ending is an important part of world history."

Rachel K. Gillette

LAWYER AND ADVOCATE

"Believe in yourself before you believe in anything else."

THE PATH TO success in the blossoming cannabis space is not an easy one and few understand this as well as Rachel K. Gillette—who has become one of the most sought after lawyers in the cannabis industry. While most people who have worked with Rachel know her for being a tenacious, driven, and compassionate attorney, her journey leading up to finding success in cannabis was far from glamorous. Rachel graduated from high school in 1992 and, shortly after, moved to Durango, Colorado, to pursue her college education and love of mountain biking. It was during her time in Durango that she learned more about the (then very illegal) process of growing marijuana. "I always saw the plant as a natural, relatively safe alternative compared to the other drugs that my peers were doing—including alcohol. I never understood why it was treated as a Schedule I substance."

Rachel attempted college, but quickly dropped out, sold all of her belongings, and, in a move surprising to those who know her, packed up and headed for Telluride, CO. It was there where she eventually had her two children and a marriage she describes as "brief." When her marriage ended, Rachel had virtually no financial support from anyone, so she started searching for ways to care for her children as a struggling single mother. "I began working as a cleaning lady. I was literally cleaning toilets to make ends meet." Once her youngest son reached school age, Rachel repacked and relocated the family to Boulder, CO where she applied to complete her schooling at the University of Colorado–which was conveniently located across the street from her eldest son's high school. She "saved her pennies" and eventually finished college, graduating with a BA in political science from the University of Colorado Boulder—at the age of 30. "All through college, I remained passionate about cannabis and the legalization of cannabis. I was also a consumer—and a parent—which has always been stigmatized, especially for women and mothers. But again, I saw this plant as a much safer alternative [to] other drugs or to alcohol."

This is where Rachel's deep passion for advocacy was born. Rachel recalls a time immediately after graduating in 2007 from the Quinnipiac University School of Law in 2007—an educational pursuit she funded almost entirely on her own—where she considered what working in cannabis would look like. "If you had told me then," she says, "that I'd be able to practice in marijuana law, I would have told you that you were crazy. It would be my dream job for sure, but it was never going to happen."

The year 2007 wasn't the most ideal time to graduate from law school with a significant amount of debt, especially as a single parent. Rachel remembers the economy and job market being a mess, but felt fortunate to get hired by a tax practice in Colorado. "I had no idea, at the time, that my background in tax would come in handy when I quit my job in 2010 and decided to start representing marijuana companies," she said. When Rachel took this major risk, it was well before the state's marijuana rules and regulations were fully fleshed out. She recognized early that Colorado would be the first state to regulate a for-profit medical model, overseen by the Colorado Department of Revenue, and that no other state was operating quite that way. The opportunity was crystal clear: Rachel would take a leap of faith, get a loan from her mother, and become an attorney dedicated solely to the cannabis field. She opened her own law firm, Rachel K. Gillette, in 2010.

When asked what the conversation was like as Rachel approached her mother for a loan, Rachel remembers feeling nothing but support.

> Like me, my mother is completely self made. She is a successful businesswoman and came from nothing, always pulling herself up by her bootstraps. I knew she was supportive of my business idea or she would have refused the loan. Oddly enough, my grandfather, who was an old school sort of guy, never supported marijuana, but supported me because he saw the value in this business and the huge opportunity.

Rachel attributes much of her early success to having support from family, including her children.

> Raising middle and high school students during a time of major transition into this regulated market was certainly interesting. I

remember them coming home from school and sharing what they had learned about marijuana in D.A.R.E. I was always open with my kids about my line of work and I think that's why I can say with certainty that neither of my kids consumed marijuana in high school.

Rachel concludes, laughing, "I guess when your mom thinks something is cool, then you, as a teenager, automatically don't think it's cool!"

Her practice began to take shape in mid-2010 after months of pounding the pavement and non-stop hustling. Rachel never lost sight of the prize: that this industry had massive economic potential for her, but also that her work would help sick and suffering people gain access to their cannabis medicine.

I knew there was tremendous risk, but it was one I was willing to take because I knew it was the right thing to do. I knew what I was doing was right and what the state was doing was right.

Alongside her were dozens of marijuana startup companies applying for licenses that would allow them to operate legally in Colorado. Many of these people, according to Rachel, seemed to be risking their freedom and putting their financial futures on the line because they were so passionate about providing medicine. Rachel has a profound respect for those who entered the industry for activist reasons in addition to their commercial interests, and feels, for entrepreneurs to be successful, they "need to care about both sides."

As many companies began blossoming and preparing for licensing, Rachel recognized that most large scale law firms were not venturing into cannabis, given that the laws were still so grey. "It wasn't clear if legally, or ethically, lawyers could provide representation at the time." She also understood that many cannabis businesses needed serious help navigating the new complex laws and rules. Given the circumstances, Rachel quickly realized that she was well positioned to support small businesses entering the industry, facing far less competition than she would have encountered in a more traditional sector.

Rachel's business began growing at a tremendous rate, not simply because of the great legal counsel her practice provided, but because her commitment to the industry and compassion for patients was obvious. Rachel owned and operated her steadily expanding firm for more than six years, and remembers her feelings of unrest as she wrestled with the decisions many small business owners face during times of growth.

> I saw the growth, but it's sometimes scary to bring on more lawyers and staff—with growth comes more expense. Did I have periods of economic instability? Sure. Did I ever ask myself how I would be able to do this? Yes. But as a single mother who had once cleaned toilets without an education or a decent paying job, [the instability] couldn't get worse!

Rachel's initial efforts were critical during the passing of Amendment 64, especially in her role as the Executive Director for NORML in Colorado, which, having existed for over 40 years, is the oldest marijuana consumer activist organization. Rachel held this position for more than four years, only recently resigning because the workload became too much on top of her legal practice. Her passion for the industry has existed for decades, a passion fueled by the enthusiasm and commitment of the people she works alongside and her firm belief in the importance of the work.

In 2016, Rachel joined forces with a larger law firm, becoming a partner at Greenspoon Marder. While the decision to close down her own practice didn't come easily, Rachel was thrilled to join this particular firm. "I understood that I was unable to meet the growing needs of the sophisticated clients walking in my door as a solo practitioner, even with one to two lawyers on staff. It was the growth of the industry that inspired me to go with a larger firm." As part of Greenspoon Marder, Rachel works with a team of attorneys who can support a much broader spectrum of cannabis law services, including regulatory compliance, real estate, intellectual property, corporate finance, and tax. "You need so many tools in your arsenal," she explains, "that for me to think that I could handle it all was not realistic. I knew if I had the resources of a larger firm, and the lawyers that came with the firm, I could keep supporting our clients." Rachel had previously been courted by several large scale law firms, but was, by far, the most impressed by Greenspoon Marder. "Greenspoon didn't just want to get into cannabis law in a quiet, secretive way. They were willing to pour resources into a cannabis group so we can truly serve the types of clients who are now getting into this industry. They were willing to be public and out front about their commitment to cannabis, while many other firms wanted to be involved more quietly."

When it comes to how gender has affected her journey within the cannabis industry, Rachel speaks clearly and candidly about her experience as a woman in the professional sphere.

Is it difficult being an attorney and a woman? Absolutely. But this has nothing to do with cannabis. Bottom line: there is an attitude in the legal community which discounts the contributions and skills of female attorneys. I don't know how many times I've had male attorneys say something to me that I know they would never say to a male counterpart attorney. One time, I was sitting in an IRS office and actually had an attorney ask me if I was "always this aggressive." There is no way he would have said that to me if I was a male. In the legal profession, women are still up against deep rooted barriers. The profession's history is entirely dominated by men. Thankfully more women graduate from law school now than men do, so I think we will see a shift.

As it relates to cannabis, Rachel is optimistic that the industry will continue to be an exceptional place for women to begin or continue their careers. As she sees it, the marijuana industry presents an outstanding opportunity for women. "It's a nascent industry that is evolving and developing at a time when women have stronger voices than they have had in the past, whether it's a business community, in society at large, or as mothers." Beyond getting involved in the industry, though, Rachel feels strongly that women need to use this opportunity to shape and mold the system so it does not slide backwards into antiquated ways of thinking and working, where men dominate and women struggle to be treated equally. To do this, she urges that women need to look out for themselves from the beginning. Her advice, not surprisingly, is for women to begin by getting themselves an attorney. "You have to make sure your voice is heard. I've seen women in this industry have trouble even being heard by their own partners. You have to have someone in your corner looking out for your own personal best interest."

Rachel does not believe this issue is unique to women; many men she has worked with have also faced similar challenges with business partners or during high level negotiations. Unfortunately, Rachel feels that, women tend to be more trusting, and as a result, they are in a riskier position than men and need to be more alert and aware. "It's been illustrated by [the 2016] election. We still live in a sexist society. It exists. Nothing saddens me more than to know that our country finds it somewhat acceptable that our leader can treat women the way Mr. Trump has." With that in mind, Rachel shares the same lecture she shares with all of her new clients: "Do not believe a word from anyone in this industry. Your lawyer has a professional duty to tell you the truth and to tell you what the law says. Your consultant does not. The guy selling you something does not. Be trusting, but verify everything so you are not taken advantage of."

The road ahead looks bright for Rachel, particularly as Greenspoon Marder begins expanding into new states and energizing markets. Her work is constantly evolving and she is confident that the brightest moments for her, as it relates to the cannabis industry, lie ahead. Rachel is a person who wakes up everyday anxious to get started and excited by the challenges she will face. She truly believes she has "the most interesting job" and feels blessed to be doing something that she loves. "This is history in the making," she says excitedly, "women should absolutely get involved." She offers some sage advice to women specifically, suggesting that the best tool one has is to "believe in yourself before you believe in anything else." She adds

I have always been an intelligent woman, but people wouldn't listen to me without an education or a degree; I was just as smart when I was cleaning toilets as I am today, but no one was going to listen to what I had to say without the credentials behind me. Education is very important, but that can come from life experience too—persistence, dedication, and getting in there and getting your hands dirty.

She suggests that women get involved by asking questions and asking others *how* they can learn. "Someone isn't going to get experience by reading a book (no offense!)—it's going to come from getting out there and learning from your peers and the people who have experienced things that you have not."

Rachel K. Gillette dreams big. She is optimistic about the future and eager to see the federal government change their outdated position on marijuana and whether it will be regulated by states or on a national level. In her ideal future, she hopes to sit down with federal regulators so she may impart her wisdom from lessons learned through trial and error in states like Colorado. The scientific research side of the business, out of which many medical opportunities will arise, excites Rachel, and she anticipates that these opportunities will expand nationally as well as internationally.

There are so, so many problems caused by prohibition. Colorado, and people who worked through legalization in Colorado, have an obligation to share these lessons with the government and with many other governments so these big picture problems may be diminished. I know we can save a lot of lives by ending the

War on Drugs. Do I have a big vision? Sure I do. But I'm optimistic and want to participate in the rethinking of international drug policy.

———

Betty Aldworth

EXECUTIVE DIRECTOR OF STUDENTS
FOR SENSIBLE DRUG POLICY

"I will never forget in my entire life how it felt to announce to the world on TV that Colorado had just legalized and regulated marijuana . . . it was the most surreal and the most real thing at the same time."

BETTY ALDWORTH'S CANNABIS career is rooted in a life long passion for advocacy, community outreach, and volunteer engagement. Her commitment to the cannabis movement began in 2009 when she first transitioned out of her full-time role managing large volunteer programs in Denver's mainstream nonprofit world, to the realm of analytical testing laboratories. Since then, she has held various positions within the industry, led numerous campaigns supporting marijuana legalization, given one of the first talks about the importance of women in the industry and, perhaps most notably, paved the way for students—many of whom are either women or minorities—to effect change on a national level through her work as Executive Director of Students for Sensible Drug Policy—self-described on their website as "an international, grassroots, student-led organization working to end drug prohibition." Betty is incredibly unique in that she has been successful, and highly influential, as both a businesswoman *and* activist, demonstrating the importance of both circles of people and the two worlds finding common ground.

Entering into cannabis happened "entirely by chance," when Betty was between jobs on an "accidental sabbatical." She remembers her nextdoor neighbor sharing that he was going to open an analytical testing laboratory for the cannabis industry and asking her if she "might be interested in assisting him with the build out process with demolition, light construction, plumbing, and runs to Home Depot." She joined this neighbor a few days later, in the summer of 2009, to start the work. Betty was fascinated and they found that her background in volunteer program management, some of which focused on healthcare, was relevant to this type of work. Before the day ended, Betty had secured herself a role as the VP of Communications and Business Development and began work immediately. "Oh, and I never made a run to Home Depot," she laughs. Betty recalls feeling "lucky," sharing: "I had a moment—a true flash of very unusual flexibility—where I had time to do whatever I wanted. I come from a working class background and had a small safety net at this time—not a lot, but enough to take a chance—which I never had before. It was that small safety net that allowed me to do this and jump in. It was literally perfect timing."

While working at the lab, Betty was influential in helping the company to scale by educating the cannabis community on the importance of testing their products for safety, quality, and potency. "We were the second lab to open in the country and had a number of great allies. It was becoming more and more clear to people that testing was a pretty important piece of the puzzle." Betty fell in love with her work, specifically speaking with community members and educating others in the space. It is the nature of work she has always been drawn to and, for nine months, she leveraged her background and skill set to translate relatively unknown science between the community and the lab. After almost a year, Betty left the laboratory and pivoted into a consulting position where she could focus all of her time and energy on community engagement and education. While she certainly enjoyed the work she was doing on her own, Betty was growing frustrated and began wondering if the work would sustain her full time. It was becoming more and more apparent to her that many people in the industry were not interested in "the soft side work" that she was doing with policy. "I wasn't able to move forward in a way that was satisfying to me and I started to think it was time to jump back out of the industry to return to my work in the nonprofit world."

At this time, on the verge of exiting the cannabis sector, Betty received a phone call from her industry colleague Jill Lamoureux. "Jill called me to see if I would join her group and begin doing some community work for her." With her mind nearly made up about leaving the world of cannabis, Betty did what many do when facing a tough decision: she flipped a coin.

It's something I do . . . I was truly not sure about how to proceed so I decided to flip a coin. The funny thing is that it's not really about what side lands face up; when I flip the coin I really listen to myself and, most of the time, have an immediate reaction to the coin toss, either excitement or disappointment, leading me to the right answer.

Betty doesn't recall how the coin landed, but knows that the process guided her toward the right path. About a week later, she joined Jill and continued her advocacy work in cannabis.

Betty worked as a consultant on Jill's team for a while. She eventually found herself at a volunteer party for Amendment 64 in Colorado. While at the event, Betty was chatting with Steve Fox, who shared with her that the Marijuana Policy Project had just posted a new job opening and that the selected candidate would be leading the women's outreach work for the Amendment 64 campaign. He encouraged Betty to apply and, soon after, she received the offer. Once again, she was leveraging her background in volunteer management and political organizing, this time at the forefront of Colorado's legalization movement, as a voice and liaison for female voters. Betty knew that having a woman spearheading this crusade would be important.

> They needed a woman's face on the campaign because suburban women in particular, who vote at very high rates, were generally opposed to cannabis at that point—although we felt then that these women could be moved on their positions if they were educated by a relatable female figure.

Betty is not a soccer mom, but jokes that she "played one on TV" and enabled women to hear reform arguments from a surprising new messenger. At the time of the 2012 campaign, it was not common to see a woman in her late thirties on television talking about cannabis *unless* she was talking about her fears surrounding legalization. Betty, on the other hand, was very vocal about why prohibition had failed and how regulation was a better answer.

The campaign's leaders, Mason Tvert, Executive Director of SAFER, and Brian Vicente, Executive Director of Sensible Colorado, had admirably represented cannabis reform for nearly a decade in Colorado, but weren't able to connect with women the way a different, more approachable representative could. During the evaluation process after the campaign, Betty and her team reviewed the numbers and, sure enough, the biggest shift had happened with suburban women.

> I will never forget in my entire life how it felt to announce to the world on TV that Colorado had just legalized and regulated marijuana—and then turning around to see all of these faces of people I care deeply about waiting to see what came next. I threw my fist the air and everyone went crazy. It was the most surreal and the most real thing at the same time.

Prior to the election, Betty had heard from the Co-Founder of The National Cannabis Industry Association, Aaron Smith, who tapped her to be the Deputy Director and NCIA's first hire. She chuckles a bit, saying, "I think Aaron saw the value in bringing on a fiery, outspoken woman to be his counterpart at NCIA. We used to joke around that, between the two of us, we covered almost all the bases the organization needed to have covered, experientially and ideologically." She was hired to build the Educational Programs division for NCIA and develop media relations. Betty went straight to work launching an educational panel series, involving NCIA in more conferences, and finding ways to engage more women in the movement.

> In 2012, the first Marijuana Business Daily conference was held in Denver and there were about 200 people in the room. I was asked to be on the marketing panel and I remember it being myself and three men. I was glad they put me up there—it was smart that they were paying attention to the number of women featured on panels in the beginning. I spent that time talking about why women were incredibly important in our work, but also as consumers.

Betty shared examples of subpar ads where "women had been turned into props," wearing next to nothing and posing suggestively. She also offered information about women from the healthcare standpoint, pointing out that "women are far more likely to suffer from chronic illnesses, far more likely to turn to natural medicine versus western medicine. Women are precisely the people you need to be talking to, so why are you alienating them, telling them this product is for men with the imagery of naked women?"

Throughout 2013, Betty played a big part in shaping the conversation about cannabis on a national scale.

> Once Colorado and Washington passed [laws regulating adult use of cannabis], states all over the country really wanted to learn more. I truly saw the industry at that time as a vector for national reform. In Colorado, we had already demonstrated, via our regulated medical program, that adult-use cannabis really wasn't scary. Bad things were not happening, and that contributed to Amendment 64's success.

As part of her role at NCIA, Betty was charged with organizing the Women's Cannabis Business Network (WCBN), previously supported by NCIA member and entrepreneur Christie Lunsford. With inadequate support at NCIA, WCBN eventually gave rise to Women Grow, founded by Amy Dannemiller (who is known more commonly by her alias, Jane West) in 2014.

> When Jane West came along, NCIA didn't have the capacity to build out the Women's Network further. The group hadn't evolved to where it could have; it had turned into a social support group where women were getting together to talk about their challenges—something that was very necessary and helpful at the time, but still not as advanced as the Network could have been. The community was important, but it needed to be taken to the next level.

Though the work at NCIA was challenging and exciting, Betty was intrigued by an invitation to interview for the role of Executive Director for SSDP (Students for Sensible Drug Policy). Betty laughs as she shares that she believes she is the "right 40-year-old" to be leading the organization. Betty has been in this role for three years and describes herself as a "tool of the students," a description she is absolutely on board with.

> I very genuinely value their voices. I strongly admire our youth, and want them to be able to represent their own priorities. Young people are our future and SSDP is always 10 years ahead of what's happening now. They are so focused on what's next and so dissatisfied with the world right now the way it is. . . . I'm very good with handling the administration, keeping the ship together, and making sure the cargo our students need is on board while our students steer us forward.

Her track record in cannabis reveals a pattern: wherever Betty worked or volunteered, she contributed in ways that especially helped women—by helping women to have a voice, educating women about cannabis and cannabis reform, or by supporting organizations like NCIA and WCBN. However, she will arguably have the most impact, in terms of creating opportunities for women and minorities, in her role as Executive Director for SSDP.

> At SSDP 48% of our participants identify as women, 4% identify as genderqueer, and 27% of leadership identifies as people of color. That representation is surprisingly [more] diverse, across a several spectra, than the reform movement is generally perceived. SSDP is giving voice to those who, historically, have not had one in the policy reform movement. My biggest challenge as ED is to balance our history, where many of our elders are cis hetero white men, and our future—which is far more diverse. I think the organization wanted someone in this role who could grapple with these [issues] and I hope to continue doing that.

When asked how other women, who are either currently operating in the industry or considering becoming involved, can continue working towards policy change and gender equality, Betty shares that all of us, men and women alike, need to be the force of change. She stresses the importance of staying involved in the movement and cultivating allies. "I particularly celebrate those entrepreneurs who began as activists; we are a movement first and an industry second." For women to truly reach parity in any field, it will take male allies recognizing their role in lifting women beyond the theoretical ceiling.

Different change modalities require different types of actors. Incremental change, which occurs most frequently in societies with reasonably stable economies and, as opposed to revolutionary change, requires individuals in power to relinquish it to those who do not have it. Education of sympathetic power-holders turns those people into allies: we must teach them that the system is unjust, that there is an imbalance of power, and that it is a moral imperative to share their power and support systemic change through elevation of marginalized voices and centering the concerns of the most marginalized in their platforms. The drug policy reform movement and the cannabis industry reflect the cultural norm of majority male power-holders in all phases—business and politics in particular. Male allies who understand that power imbalance impedes everyone's progress and who are ready to elevate the norm by sharing their power with women, accelerate the pace toward equity. It takes the web that we weave together to create a change we can all be proud of.

After decades of slow, but steady, progress followed by a confounding election, we have to mount an effective opposition. The people are ready for reform and the administration will push back in every way: they want to deport immigrants, and are decidedly anti-science, anti-compassion, and anti-human-rights toward drug users. We need allies with us now because we have a lot of good progress to defend, but a lot of progress that still needs to be made.

Betty Aldworth feels she has her future work cut out for her as she battles the current federal administration for policy reform. It is her hope that SSDP and the cannabis movement as a whole will continue to cultivate male and female allies alike to join her in enacting the peaceful change that is so necessary in America today. Cannabis reform will continue to be her primary focus, and, as Betty reflects on her career, she is grateful for her "incredibly special" journey to SSDP.

My entire career has been random opportunities that magically coalesce all of these things I enjoy doing and things I am good at into a delightful package. I was able to participate in very small ways in a variety of very strong social movements in my lifetime, and cannabis is one of them. I love the issue and I love the work. I'm here now because, through my work in marijuana, I have developed and strengthened my view that [The War on Drugs] is the foundation on which a variety of social ills are built. I am here as a human rights advocate, and cannabis reform is a critically important set of policies that needs changing. The cannabis industry is a necessary byproduct—America needs and wants something other than the illicit market.

Susan Squibb

CANNABIS MAVEN AND FOUNDER
OF MOTHER'S HIGH TEA

"If I were going to feel limited, those limits were of my own creation; if I could dream it, I could do it, and the only thing in my way was me."

"MOST OF MY adult life has been in the cannabis space." There is no tone of boasting or self-importance when Susan Squibb recounts her journey through two decades as an activist, hemp and marijuana legalization advocate, and cannabis entrepreneur. Susan is a trailblazer, who enjoys developing innovative hemp products for health food markets. She has worked on virtually all stages of the Colorado's marijuana initiative campaigns as either a paid employee or volunteer. Today, she continues to promote informed conversation through her advice column at *The Cannabist* and fosters a strong community of women in the cannabis industry with her annual social event, Mother's High Tea. From campaigning for Colorado's Amendment 20 that legalized medical marijuana in 2000, to working on Safer Alternative For Enjoyable Recreation initiatives for the city of Denver and across the state from 2005 through 2007, to fighting for the passage of Amendment 64 that legalized the recreational use of marijuana in Colorado in 2012, Susan has worked on it all. Considering that her efforts led, first, to the two Denver initiatives passing and, eventually, the legalization of adult possession of up to an ounce of marijuana across the state while also making marijuana the lowest priority for police, she is confoundingly humble when telling her story.

For Susan, the cannabis movement has been a calling since she was 20 years old, but even growing up, she describes herself as very conscious and driven. She was an honor student, a Girl Scout, and a vegetarian, and found her way into cannabis while studying for an anthropology degree at the University of Colorado Boulder. Before the semester started, she recalls, "I was walking in Denver and there was a man selling hemp cookies out of a basket right on the street." She laughs, "I certainly needed some explanation before I agreed to try one, mainly that it was not going to get me high, and I became intrigued by the story!" Susan started to learn about this sweet tasting hemp cookie, the nutritious qualities of hemp seed, and the political challenges the plant faced due to prohibition.

The man with the basket was a character named Agua Das (Susan confirms that, yes, that is his real name), with whom Susan first became friends and, later, partners. The two started baking and selling hemp cookies, not only on the street "Shakedown Street" style, but also with vending booths at events. "To me, how a company did business was as important as the products they were selling. I was really inspired by companies like Ben & Jerry's and The Body Shop, who had triple bottom lines *and* cared about the community, whether global, local, or environmental." Susan saw Agua Das's cookies as an opportunity for a community activism project, to raise awareness about the laws surrounding not only hemp, but marijuana. "I was involved with the cookies for 15 years and, eventually, the hemp cookies turned into hemp ice cream [Hemp I Scream!] and hemp ice cream sandwiches." In 1998 and 1999, as well as from 2004 to 2010, Susan had a subcontract with the City and County of Denver, selling her Hemp I Scream! goodies at Red Rocks Amphitheatre, a breathtaking outdoor venue with a capacity of nearly 10 thousand people. She sold her treats at over 200 concerts and still cites the experiences she had with the concert-goers at the amphitheatre as a career highlight.

> Those people were there to see their bands and not to learn about hemp, marijuana, or counter-culture; I brought that to mainstream audiences . . . an incredible opportunity that I loved and cherished so much. It was a great way for me to interact with people and I fielded so many questions that it really fueled my advice column and made me want to continue the conversation and continue educating the people that were curious about these issues.

At Red Rocks, Susan discovered that changing the hearts and minds of individuals and shifting paradigms starts with conversation. "It can be everyday people talking about it, and then at some point it becomes a more legislative conversation, and the conversation elevates to people in positions of power who can do things." Susan currently keeps the conversation elevated through her marijuana advice column, "Ask The Cannabist," for *The Denver Post*'s online marijuana website, *The Cannabist*. The column serves as a platform for her to "discuss and solve readers' problems on marijuana related issues and assist the societal transformation from illicit use to appropriate use through expert recommendations and current data." Readers of her advice enjoy a variety of topics ranging from drug testing, proper dosing of homemade edibles, and parental advice, ("Help! My 13-year-old is Smoking Marijuana") to news on legislation, emerging markets, and even amusing questions of practicality and logistics ("Can I Take Scooby While I Shop for a Doobie?").

Another important focus very near and dear to Susan's heart is the elaborate community social event, Mother's High Tea, which she has produced since 2011 through her event production company 4 & 20 Blackbirds. The event came about as a unique way to pay tribute to her mother, who passed away from ovarian cancer in 2010, by "carrying on her legacy of community involvement." Susan shares,

> I do not come from a supportive family, *except for my mother.* My mother was always encouraging of me, even though she may not have agreed personally with the path that I've chosen—as mothers tend to worry—she just wanted to know that I would be okay, stay safe, and care for myself. She didn't always agree with me person- ally, but she always encouraged my exploration and my indepen- dence. She passed away in 2010, and so with her passing, largely the support from the rest of my family disappeared at that time as well.

Susan mentions that her former sister-in-law continues to be a voice of encouragement and support. Mother's High Tea celebrates the business- women and advocates of the cannabis community, inviting them to dress up, get together, have fun, and hear speakers share inspiring, smart, and moving stories at an "upscale and feminine event."

As she speaks about the lack of support from the majority of her family members, Susan confides,

> When I got my position as the freelance writer at *The Cannabist*, my stepmother said it was the "most embarrassing thing" and that she was mortified that I would be writing a marijuana advice

column for such a large newspaper. Also, when I first started writing in 2013 for THC Magazine, I started a column called "Ask Lady Cannabis" and I remember asking my brother for a list of questions. He shut me down. My brother said he had no questions, that he knew everything he wanted and needed to know about marijuana, and he actually persuaded my niece to disengage with me. She was a teenager at the time and he didn't want her talking to me because of my involvement with marijuana.

Despite the withdrawal and judgement she felt from her own family, Susan believes communication and dialogue is essential to navigating the changes to the laws and social beliefs surrounding cannabis.

Susan is one tough cookie, but she still admits, "Not having that family support has impacted me and my confidence." Because she has dedicated her life to legalizing and mainstreaming cannabis, she feels her family sees only her alternative lifestyle and not her successes. "They see me as an underfunctioning little sister rather than an independent person who's making her own choices that don't revolve around marrying, owning a house, or having children." In order to get through the tough aspects of working in the often misunderstood cannabis industry, Susan says she relies on her friends for support and encouragement.

> Everyday is not easy. There are a lot of highs and a lot of lows. The most difficult part is rebounding when things get rough. This is a very tumultuous space—when things don't go the way I'd like them to go, I ask, "What do I do now? What do I do next?" Fortunately, I have built a community of people who know and understand me and what I'm trying to accomplish, and they recognize my good intentions and they see me as more of a full person. I am successful. I am completely comfortable and driven in what I do. I wish my family was more understanding of me and could see that too. I am working in a dynamic field and I feel very fulfilled in what I do.

Susan has a long list of some of the most important women, men, and companies who serve as her guiding lights and fill that familial void. For inspiration "outside of cannabis," she looks to Anita Roddick of The Body Shop, Yvon Chouinard of Patagonia, Ben & Jerry's, Oprah, Madonna, Martha Stewart, and Hillary Rodham Clinton. She is grateful for the mentorship and moral support of colleagues both local to Colorado—Betty Aldworth, Kristi Kelly, Wanda James, Diane Fornbacher, Christie Lunsford, Toni Fox—and from Seattle—Ah Warner, AC Braddock, Alison Draisin. Susan also cites Debby Goldsberry, Elvy Musikka, Doreen Bishop, and Brownie Mary Rathbun as dauntless "medical activist pioneers" as well as Joy Beckerman, Anndrea Hermann, Lynda Parker for being her "hemp heros."

Fortunately for the marijuana movement and for the industry, Susan is steadfast in her activism and groundbreaking work. She converts her pain and frustration to energy, powering her forward on her mission to shatter the stereotypes of females in cannabis and of the plant itself. Susan recalls,

> The first hint that society at large was intrigued by women advocating for legalization—or having cannabis businesses—was back in 2009. At that time, I was part of the Women's Marijuana Movement, a project of Safer Alternative For Enjoyable Recreation, and the organization would host press conferences. Those press conferences would get so much media traction and created a spark in the media relating to women. There was something about women, who typically hold the keys to normalcy in society—sort of the "mother knows best" concept—advocating for something that was illegal, that shocked mainstream audiences.

The realization that she could have a truly meaningful impact as a woman in the cannabis space lit a spark that excited Susan to keep forging ahead; to fill what she perceived as a great need for women in the movement to legalize cannabis. "I saw the stereotypes surrounding advocates for legalization, and I saw that in my embodiment as a woman, I represented a different perspective and a different face from what people expected. They don't expect an honor student-Girl Scout to be advocating for legalization!"

Susan blames the continued existence of gender roles in our society for holding females back from breaking the glass ceiling, though she thinks women may have a *slight* advantage as it pertains to the grass ceiling of cannabis.

> It really depends on the company, as to how they treat women; I think it's difficult for women in the business space, period. At Hemp Sources, Inc., where I was president of the company, I was attracted to the hemp cookies and ice cream, but also to the feeling that, if I were going to feel limited, those limits were of my own creation; if I could dream it, I could do it, and the only thing in my way was me. Since then, I see the cannabis business still struggling with the same gender roles our society struggles with, and that women who are independent, I think, have a much harder time than women who run businesses with their husbands or family. Women will have an easier time succeeding if they are in a supportive environment. Ultimately, women in roles of influence makes a company stronger and more resilient.

Women have a harder time, she believes, because they "are not encouraged to be aggressive." Susan perceives that, in a nascent industry where the rules are still being created, it seems to be that the aggressive personalities get more traction and move forward faster, but "aggressive women are not seen in the most positive light." It is her feeling that "women get left out because of the way men and women were raised in society." With the rise in women's general awareness as it pertains to cannabis, Susan observes that there is a higher percentage of females in senior roles within the space. She acknowledges,

There is an understanding that women are needed to normalize this, but because the rules and the dynamics have not quite been settled, it's not an even playing field. It's such a tumultuous industry; the change really is constant. I think that as more, larger companies become interested in investing in this space, that they are bringing on new people and maybe haven't recognized the importance of women in this.

Her contributions to cannabis have been, and continue to be, invaluable. Still, Susan divulges,

I've experienced times where I wait to be included in things, and that inclusion never comes. It's an issue I think a lot of women face. Men, if they are not aware, can stay in a comfort zone and only hire or work with other men because they, ultimately, don't know how to treat a woman or create an inclusive workplace. It's necessary for inclusion and good work practice to have job and project guidelines, clear expectations, and good communication. This can be sadly missing in cannabis companies. It's crucial for women to speak up and advocate for themselves. If women aren't involved in the friend-of-a-friend approach to creating networks of support, they are getting left out. Cronyism is huge. Opportunities are often landed because of someone you know. This is some of the initial reasoning behind Mother's High Tea, because there was a need for an event that brought women in cannabis together—a social event. It is important for women to create their own networks of support and community to help stay included in the conversation.

Susan views this as an unfortunate reality modern day women face, that "they have to be very aware of the double standard of aggressive behavior versus being *nice* or *too soft*; creating your own community is one way to be supported and included." To those women considering making an entrance into the cannabis industry, Susan advises,

Do a lot of research. Find a niche or service that isn't being provided. Certainly this industry needs more professionalism and advanced business services to grow. It's not a typical industry; we don't have consistent banking, we need a lot of technological support, and there are a lot of gaps that need to be filled. I also think it's important for any woman getting into the industry to make an income and not jump in with blind faith. As much as the media likes to share stories of women entrepreneurs being successful, it doesn't showcase the frustration, failures, or the dark side of how this industry can chew people up and spit them out.

There is more than one way to be successful in cannabis. I notice a number of colleagues who, like myself, maintain multiple avenues of income and don't always rely on one thing. Don't jump in with a wild idea and hope everything will work out. *The fantasies of this industry's potential can sting you in reality.*

For this reason she further urges, *"Get it in writing.* Have some pretty standard employment agreements, operating agreements, service contracts, etc. There are a lot of handshake deals and verbal agreements and it can be very complicated if things get misunderstood," a sentiment echoed by most of the women interviewed for this project.

Susan takes a few seconds to reflect on several highlights of her own career, some of which, she admits, "have been significant to me, but not necessarily to the movement." For example, she exclaims, "I once got a signed response from the DEA Administrator, Asa Hutchinson, to a letter I had sent to them in protest! I was pretty excited to get that." Additionally, Susan was a caregiver to the first patient on the Colorado Medical Marijuana Registry. "It was an honor to help a patient, to be there and to be of service to him, at the beginning of the program." She also spotlights her freelance writing gig with *The Cannabist*, declaring that "it has been a real treasure seeing my columns on the front page of the online *Denver Post.*" She adds, "In my heart, I have many proud moments and highlights over the past 20 years. I like to live an interesting life and I enjoy the possibilities of here and now. I am excited about new opportunities in the future."

One of Susan's unique qualities is that she exudes an aura of laid-back levelheadedness. The struggles with her family and the rocky road of her formidable career have, perhaps, resulted in her adoption of a persona quite different from the more enthusiastic women who have arrived in the space more recently. In this fashion, her plans for the future are pragmatic and pay homage to her roots. "I'm going to continue developing Mother's High Tea, as I really enjoy the event and creating that community. I'll be jumping back into school to get a paralegal certificate and sharpen some skills for a legal profession. Everything in cannabis is related to law—I see that as a really good additional skill." In pursuit of her next role, she is also considering relocating to a new state or a new country, specifically to pursue her passion for the developing wellness market and for high quality and non-psychoactive phytocannabinoid products. "I want to go back into a hemp food company or nutraceutical company. I want to see cannabis wellness products available in health food stores at affordable prices."

Susan attributes much of her success in this space to her persistent questioning and her words are frequently reminiscent of JFK's: "Ask not what your country can do for you, ask what you can do for your country." Susan continues to ask herself: "What is needed now? Not only for myself and for my business, but for the industry, for mainstreaming, and for the movement. How do we keep the goals of social justice issues, that initially inspired a lot of people to want to change the laws, active and on the front burner—rather than having business run over that?" The answers to her questions are sometimes elusive and often fickle, but Susan Squibb will continue to ask and continue to influence.

———

Karin Lazarus

Founder and CEO of Sweet Mary Jane

"You should find your passion, find what you love, and do that. Stick with that."

FOR THE BETTER part of her life, Karin Lazarus was passionate about baking. It began when she was a little girl; making chocolate chip cookies using a recipe from a kid's cookbook her mother had given to her. As she got older, she started to experiment with flavors, and baking developed into a fervent hobby. In high school, Karin recalls making a sweet bread using rose petals from her backyard: "It was a hit, and I began selling it to shops in New York." As an adult, Karin poured the majority of her spare time and energy into trying new recipes and baking for her friends. At this time, she was living in New York City and working as an art representative, but was always looking for an opportunity to spend a few hours in the kitchen or pick up a catering gig on the side. However, baking was always her favorite activity. While Karin genuinely enjoyed her job in New York City's fine arts scene, she knew that she didn't feel the same type of love for her work that she did for baking and the culinary arts. It was time for a change.

Soon after, she and her husband, Charley, decided to move to the British Virgin Islands where he built luxury homes and Karin catered for people who were chartering yachts. They lived there for 10 years. While living in Tortola, they learned that they were pregnant, and after their daughter, Lucienne, was born, they moved back to NYC to be be closer to family. When they decided they didn't want to raise their daughter in the city, the couple began exploring other options, eventually agreeing that Colorado would be the right fit. In 1993, they packed their bags and headed west to try out a new lifestyle, far from their families and support systems back in New York. Karin and Charley were able to find jobs upon their arrival and Karin began working to develop recipes for a healthy-lifestyle magazine. While she was grateful for the opportunity she, once again, found herself yearning to bake professionally. "After a while, the job at the magazine was just not satisfying, I decided to go to the Caribbean to spend some time thinking about what I wanted to do with my life. We have family ties there so it was an easy trip for me to make and I thought, if I had a little time to think and consider my options, I might have more clarity back in Colorado."

While on vacation, Karin received news that helped her see, even more clearly, that she needed to focus on her baking. "Before I went on my trip, I had entered the TuttiFoodie [and] Scharffen Berger Chocolate Adventure Contest for my Chocolate-Filled Pandan Dumplings and I was delighted to learn, while on the trip, that I had won the grand prize! It wasn't a lot of money, but as I considered what to do with it, it became very clear. I was going to take the money and open a bakery."

So, in 2009, Karin developed her business plan for the bakery. Interestingly enough, Karin's journey into cannabis began at the same time. As she was evaluating her options for the new bakery, she also started reading a lot about cannabis because it was starting to be featured in the news. It wasn't long before Karin connected the dots and decided that this bakery should produce beautiful, delicious, cannabis-infused treats. This twist was exactly the edge she felt she needed.

It is important to note that, as Karin began contemplating a cannabis bakery, the Colorado market was not yet regulated; however, there was a legal medical marijuana marketplace. "At this time, with few regulations, we weren't on Metrc tracking products or inventory. You could just go to a dispensary, show them what you had, and make the sale." Metrc was developed by a company called Franwell, and was designed to track inventory in Colorado's regulated market. It was first introduced in December 2013 and is now used to create tracking and transparency for plants and products from seed to sale. Prior to Metrc and formal regulations, the industry operated very differently than it does today.

Karin reflects on a number of occasions where she and her fellow cannabis colleagues were operating in a brand new industry that was not yet fully regulated. Their practices were very different from those used in running a business under the stringent regulations that exist today; individuals and business owners would purchase cannabis in a much more informal way. "I remember someone I knew in the industry handed me a small amount of weed and told me to 'go home and show me what you can do,'—so I did." Karin was clever early on, striving to open a business in the most cost effective way possible stretching her prize money. She visited thrift stores to find her kitchen supplies and vividly remembers the day when she spent a mere $60 to purchase a lightly used oven that she would use to begin testing recipes in her new bakery.

Karin had used cannabis before, but not regularly, and she had only baked with cannabis a few times in college. She was obviously skilled in the baking process and familiar with the baking industry, but quickly realized there were many more hurdles and grey areas in the marijuana sphere. For a long time, she was unsuccessful at finding a property to rent where she could build out a kitchen. "I remember calling landlords and having them hang up on me. They would say things like, 'Are you crazy? We don't rent to your kind!' It was extremely difficult to find landlords in support of what I was trying to do." And it wasn't just the landlords questioning whether or not Karin was going crazy. "Many of my friends thought I had lost it!" It took some time, but eventually Karin got lucky and found a landlord willing to rent her a space.

When Karin started to talk about her plan with others, it was her parents' response that surprised her the most. Still living on the other side of the country with limited understanding as to what was going on in Colorado, it is understandable how they questioned her aspirations of being a legal cannabis baker. "Living in New York City, they could not figure out how this was remotely legal. My father thought I was going to wind up in jail! Yet, he supported me and was curious about the world I was living in. . . . He passed away in 2012 and I wish he could see where I am now. And that I'm still not in jail!"

The rest of Karin's family was also supportive, especially her daughter, Lucienne, "Lucie," who, at the time, was a sophomore at George Washington University. Lucie went on to work in her mother's business after college and, at the time of publishing, has recently become a partner. With the support of her immediate family and some friends, Karin was off to the races and had no intention of turning back. She remembers seeing a Ray Bradbury quote that truly seemed to express her mentality and process as she launched her endeavor: "'Jump off of the cliff and build your wings on the way down.'"

In 2010, many sleepless nights and incredibly long weeks later, Karin's dream business became a reality by the name of Sweet Mary Jane. "We built a wholesale bakery and we were proud of the medicated baked goods we were selling to dispensaries." Karin spent as much time as she could reading about the healing properties of cannabis, working hard to improve her formulations. It wasn't until she began hearing from patients who had purchased her products, though, that Karin really understood the power of cannabis as a medicine.

> When I started creating confections, I thought I was simply sending out delicious baked goods with cannabis in them. But then I started getting calls and emails from people who were using our products as medicine telling us how their lives had changed. And that's when [the business] changed for me. When I realized that our products were helping people, my passion for baking became something bigger. I knew I had chosen the perfect path; not only do I get to bake, I get to make a difference in a person's life.

Consistently inspired by her patients as well as her team, Karin was able to build Sweet Mary Jane into one of the most well recognized edibles companies in Colorado. Her company is distinctive because Karin has never strayed from their specialized, boutique approach. The company is known for using natural, whole foods and vibrant ingredients. Being that Sweet Mary Jane makes products to be used as medicines, Karin still feels today the way she did initially: it is important that her products are not only good tasting, but good for the consumer, as well. Sweet Mary Jane produces a wide array of desserts and handmade baked goods. From their award winning OMG! Brownie Cheesecake and Key Lime Kickers to their high potency Delta-9 6000mg THC tincture, the bakery strives for the utmost in consistency to ensure appropriate dosing for all consumers. At the THC Championship in December 2016, Sweet Mary Jane's Love at First Bite chocolates won first place as Best Edible. In addition, Karin is the author of the Sweet Mary Jane Cookbook. Her diverse team wholesales these delectable edibles all over the state of Colorado.

Business has been good for Karin and she feels extremely lucky to have a career that she loves so much. For Karin, her current success in this industry represents the culmination of many small battles she had to fight and hurdles she had to surmount along her journey. She recognizes that many other women creating businesses at the same time overcame similar challenges:

> I find it inspirational that so many women were brave enough to step into this industry when things were super hard . . . when no one knew what the industry was like and what was ahead of us. We had no history to look back on, we are the ones creating that history. Women went in when it was tough and that's why I think they have been so powerful in the cannabis world. We began when there was no information, a far cry from those starting now, who can launch their businesses from a paved road. There are so many new brands, celebrity brands as an example, entering the industry now. But they aren't having to come in with their machetes to get their businesses open. At Sweet Mary Jane, we celebrate the industry as a whole and love the fact that it's one of the first industries driven by women. I don't feel afraid of the growth; I welcome the growth and hope to see cannabis become a more mainstream part of people's everyday lives. This plant is not something to fear.

Karin and the rest of her team at Sweet Mary Jane are committed to "dispelling this *Reefer Madness* culture to show people how beautiful cannabis can be for many different reasons, whether it [is] used for medicinal or recreational purposes." While she credits the pioneering women for their brave work early on, she is also incredibly supportive of newcomers—men and women alike—who are interested in joining the industry today. Given the strenuous nature of this work, Karin does point out that this industry is "not for the faint of heart." She emphasizes, "Newcomers need to figure out what their strengths are, develop an idea, and then stick with it. Follow your gut. I have loved baking since I was a little girl and there were a number of times in my life where I ignored that passion to pursue something else. You should find your passion, find what you love, and do that. Stick with that."

Karin doesn't simply encourage involvement with her words. She actively mentors others in a hands-on way, and is a self described "open book" when good people with good intentions come to her with questions. Coincidentally, another woman interviewed during the drafting of this book relayed an experience she had with Karin; this woman is developing a marijuana bakery near her home in Canada and, hungry for information, reached out to Karin in the form of a cold-call to ask if there was any way the two could meet. To her surprise, Karin not only took her phone call, but invited her to come spend a few weeks in Colorado observing the Sweet Mary Jane team in their Boulder facility so she could see firsthand what goes into operating a cannabis-infused edibles business. Karin explains, saying, "I wanted to help her out. She was so kind, sweet, eager to learn and I could see she had a lot of compassion. I always want to share the knowledge that I have gained over the years because I remember a time when there was no one for me to turn to for help."

The legalization of either recreational or medical marijuana in many states brought about during the 2016 election has resulted in a barrage of people hoping to get into the cannabis industry. Karin has been approached by many to expand into these new markets, but is cautious about growing outside of Colorado too quickly.

Karin is an ideal mentor because she has had to navigate extreme highs and lows, but does not let the turbulence distract her. She is appreciative of the highlights in her career, and approaches the rough patches with courage and grit. She recalls a time when Sweet Mary Jane had been open for about two years and her kitchen was raided.

I had no idea that the property belonging to my landlord was being watched by the DEA. One day, six men came into our kitchen with machine guns and broke our door down. They had come in the wrong door, without a warrant apparently, thinking they were going into my landlord's grow. They destroyed much of the kitchen and, of course, this really shook all of us up. I was not compensated for damages as I never asked to be. That did not feel like a road I wanted to go down! I'm sure you can understand why. I remember thinking, "Oh my God, I am in an industry where something like this can happen."

The raid ultimately had nothing to do with Karin, nor was this situation unique to Karin. Many of the pioneering men and women in cannabis have faced similar treatment due to misunderstandings. Fortunately for Karin, and many of the other small business owners in the cannabis space today, raids in Colorado are far less frequent . . . for now. However, with a new administration taking office, a period of uncertainty for the industry. Still, even with this uncertainty aside, unfamiliar challenges arise almost weekly in this new industry. For Karin, while her situation was difficult, it taught her a lot about teaming up with others and advocating for positive changes. "Your cannabis license is tied to an address, so relocating without finding approved space to lease and filling out a new application would be the end of your business. All of us [tenants] got together and approached the Marijuana Enforcement Division, asking them to give us time to relocate as we were not involved in the landlord's business in any way." By working together and fighting together, the businesses were granted an extension to find a new location to operate, so Karin reports that "things worked out, but it was a close call."

At the time of publishing, Karin is working to understand the new labeling requirements that have recently been released for all Colorado edibles companies. "Staying in compliance is of the utmost importance to us. However, I do wish there was a way for the industry and state to be more aligned in defining what this means —especially when new requirements are released." The latest changes have caused quite a bit of confusion with rule interpretation, especially for marijuana infused product companies. Still, Karin has a lot of faith that, as time goes on, state regulatory bodies will develop better systems for holding businesses accountable, releasing new requirements, and working *with* these businesses to create a better industry. She is committed to being part of the solution by providing feedback and ideas where she is able.

Today Karin and her daughter, Lucie, who "has made a world of difference in building Sweet Mary Jane," are focused on refining their operation, training new employees, and giving back however they can. Sweet Mary Jane donates 100% of the proceeds from their Creature Comfort Tincture for pets to the Wildlife Sanctuary in Colorado. The Sweet Mary Jane team is also focusing on educating patients and customers on their products, something they are deeply passionate about. "I'd like people to be learning a lot more about their products so they can better understand them and their uses. This education would extend to budtenders, and then flow to patients curious about our products. That's a challenge as a [business-to-business] company.

Karin Lazarus knows if she and her team "keep going, keep jumping through hoops of fire, with time, it will all fall into place. . . . I think it will be good for us. I'm optimistic and everyday I thank the people of Colorado who, in the spirit of freedom, have given all of us who work in this industry the opportunity to realize our dreams."

Heidi Keyes

FOUNDER OF PUFF, PASS & PAINT
CO-FOUNDER OF CANNABISTOURS.COM

"I think it's important to help the community while growing your business—I don't want to have a company that doesn't give back to the community."

Rising star Heidi Keyes, the founder of Puff, Pass & Paint (PPP), is a down-to-earth entrepreneur and artist. She is also a talented writer, famous for using Facebook to share her stories—both the highlights and the hardships—in the most comical ways. Many of Heidi's successes can be attributed to her humor. She is able to make light of the frustrations that come with a new industry and launching a startup in a relatable way that help others refocus, relax, and maybe even laugh a little. That's who Heidi is: the friend and peer who can effortlessly brighten up someone's day, instantly reminding those who have the pleasure of knowing and working with her that even the toughest days are surmountable. She is one of the people in the cannabis community who, in her unique and artistic way, helps others to regain perspective and empowers them to continue moving forward. This is exemplified clearly through her work as an instructor and business owner as she teaches others to explore their creativity and make art—while getting high.

Puff, Pass & Paint is the "first ever cannabis-friendly all-inclusive art class"[1]; attendees gather in an open-minded environment where marijuana consumption is accepted and welcomed. Men and women, both young and old (though all over the age of 21), attend her classes. Heidi points out that, while most people choose to partake by consuming cannabis throughout the class, others have come solely to check things out and paint, not consuming at all. For all of these reasons and more, Heidi has described her work as "the best job ever," and is proud to play a part in both promoting diversity within the industry and normalizing cannabis use. As more states legalize cannabis for recreational use, Heidi is growing her business while bringing together the art, tourism, and cannabis communities.

When asked where her fearlessness and entrepreneurship come from, Heidi proudly shares that she learned much of this from her parents:

I have never really been afraid of failure because I was raised by two entrepreneurs. My parents own a petting farm in our home state of Wisconsin, and, growing up, I watched them do well, but

I also watched them fail. I saw them evaluate and reevaluate—they always found a way to pivot and try something new or figure out a different way around a problem. If the business failed, they would regroup and try something else. There will always be times of struggle, but I never felt the fear of failing.

Of course, facing potential failure is never easy and can be downright scary, even for the most confident entrepreneur, but Heidi's sense of humor and grounded outlook keep her fear in check. Her intrepidness resulted in an extremely successful launch of PPP in a matter of months.

Prior to her work in cannabis, Heidi was living in Colorado working part-time as an artist and for a leasing company. Like many major cities around the US, Denver began seeing an increase in art classes that combined drinking wine and painting. One of Heidi's friends reached out to share an idea, suggesting that Heidi explore the same business model but with weed instead of wine. To Heidi, this was the perfect business concept. It married her love of making and teaching art with her love of smoking pot. Intrigued, Heidi "put a few short posts up on Facebook, trying to test the waters and gauge interest, and the response was overwhelmingly positive!" Not knowing if a business like this could function legally in Colorado, Heidi sought counsel from an attorney.

> I needed to make sure I was doing things correctly and feel that, if people in our industry *don't* spend the time and money clarifying their ideas and getting approval and counsel by legal, we can put the entire industry at risk. One person operating illegally or out of compliance can harm all of us and can undo so much hard work.

With the lawyer's approval, a little cash she'd saved, and small space she cleared in her living room, Heidi decided to go for it and began hosting classes in her own home.

The legalization of recreational marijuana in Colorado produced a brand new market of adults anxious to exercise their right to consume. It was an exciting time for Heidi as PPP took off. Heidi remarks, "We would smoke, we would paint, it was intimate and fun, and it grew so much, so quickly!" However, Heidi hit a small bump in the road even before the first easel was set: she wasn't sure how to tell her parents about her new venture.

> I remember when I scheduled my first class. I had been hiding all of my Facebook posts from my mom, but I wanted to come clean. I called her up, told her about my idea, and she said, "You're doing *what*?!" My family is from rural Wisconsin. They're not cannabis users even though I've been smoking since I was 15 years old. We have friends and family members who use medical cannabis, but my mom really had no knowledge of this before I started Puff, Pass & Paint. Once she learned I had already talked to a lawyer and that I was covered, she started to come around.

Having her mother's blessing was important to Heidi, given her mother's role in teaching her so much about entrepreneurship. Heidi wanted to have her family's support and, beyond that, wanted to continue learning from her parents. It took time, but eventually Heidi's mother and father accepted her decision as well as her viable business model. "I am so proud of [my mother] especially, and the way she has grown into this and the conversations we have. It's funny now having these conversations with someone who has never been a cannabis user."

By January 2014, dispensary doors were officially open, allowing recreational marijuana to be purchased legally. With out-of-state tourists flocking to Colorado to celebrate the state's decision to legalize, Heidi's classes began selling out. There were so many emails coming in asking Heidi to add more classes to the calendar that she outgrew the art space she had set up in her home. It was time to start looking for a more formal venue and additional teachers. After many interviews, tours of various locations, and many months of effort, Heidi brought on a second instructor, Chris, who now primarily leads the Denver PPP classes and found a new cannabis-friendly venue for the studio.

Heidi's seemingly-bottomless well of positivity is inspiring, but, as many have expressed, things in the cannabis industry aren't always as they appear. Even Heidi is not immune. She has experienced many bright moments, but persevered through some dark, murky ones, as well. In the midst of uncertainty during the first year of PPP, the company began to experience some growing pains and Heidi thought it might have been time to shut things down. "I thought: this is too hard, it should be more natural. I actually started applying to flight attendant jobs secretly, a position I had held before I began teaching art in 2013. I even went to Florida and interviewed for a few positions, but, thankfully, I didn't hear back on the job for awhile and, in the meantime, things started to swing upward."

Heidi didn't stop at this success. After tightening up her business model and assessing a number of potential business partners, Heidi linked up with Michael Eymer, founder of Colorado Cannabis Tours. In 2015, Michael sent Heidi a business proposal suggesting a merger; this expansion fused together his tour company with her existing class offerings. With Michael's support and an expanded vision for the future, Heidi set her intentions on the next phase of business: bringing their company into new states and adding additional creative mediums. Most notably, Heidi introduced Puff, Pass & Pottery as well as Puff, Pass & Pincushion and, in addition to her Denver classes, has officially launched Puff, Pass & Paint in Washington, DC, and Oregon. On January 1, 2017, the duo launched their brand new website and parent company, CannabisTours.com. Adding to her existing class offerings, Cannabis Tours has partnered with cannabis-friendly hotels and venues in Las Vegas and California where Heidi will, ultimately, host more PPP classes. Heidi never let any of the turbulence she met kill her vibe.

Beyond expanding into new markets, Heidi is conscientious about doing right by the communities she is entering, always looking to hire locally and to support local organizations. While preparing to set up shop in Las Vegas, Heidi made contact with an organization called Herbal Mothers, which is, according to Heidi, focused on supporting parents using medical marijuana by trying to educate the community and to lift a pre-existing stigma that parents who use cannabis are reckless. "I think it's important to help the communities while growing your business—I don't want to have a company that doesn't give back to the community."

Heidi freely admits many people have helped her on her journey to success, and adds that she feels being a woman and an artist has worked in her favor:

> I love being a woman in this industry. There is a great network of women who want to help one another. Jane West—who is also from Wisconsin—has been a huge support to me since the beginning. Brittney Driver and I were also introduced early on and she has become a great friend and peer. There's enough room in this industry for us all to succeed. I think there are some women who are extremely competitive, more worried about themselves than creating a network and community. But I think, as the industry expands, it's so important to have good people on your team. The instructors I have are incredible. I love making art and I love smoking weed, which has sometimes resulted in people not expecting me to be a strong business owner or negotiator with novel ideas. I have been constantly underestimated which, at times, has worked to my advantage.

The smart choices Heidi made early on in her business, combined with the help she has received from other professionals in the space—both men and women—and her drive to keep pushing onward, has enabled the growth and success of PPP and CannabisTours.com. The way the art community fosters inclusion is something Heidi would like to see translate into the cannabis sphere. She hopes other women will come into this industry and, as her own business expands, wants to keep hiring women and minorities who are already established in their local art communities. Heidi also offers sound advice to those who will be breaking into the industry: "Definitely speak to a lawyer before you do anything. Make sure you are doing things correctly as far as legalization goes. Make sure you're building a network. You can't be an island in this industry. No one is going to be able to help you if you're not helping others."

Heidi's favorite thing about teaching classes that help reduce the stigma surrounding recreational marijuana consumption is proving to people that there is *no such thing* as a "typical cannabis consumer." Watching cannabis connect people has been a true highlight of her PPP experience.

Art creates common ground. I want to continue to provide an environment where cannabis can be consumed responsibly and in a fun manner and where people are free to have an experience with someone they might not have met otherwise. In our classes, we meet a lot of people who have never tried cannabis before and this is a fun way for them to safely experiment. Additionally, at least one person in every class does not consume (consumption is encouraged, but not required), but they still see cannabis in an environment where everyone is laughing and enjoying themselves and no one is getting crazy. Even if they don't smoke, their experience is still beautiful and enjoyable.

In addition to her friends, family, and industry colleagues, Heidi credits her incredible team for helping foster PPP's continued growth.

In Portland, I have a super self-sufficient and talented instructor, Samantha Montanaro, and a woman named Stacey Mulvey is killing it for us in DC. In Denver, I have full faith in Chris Eldert and Tyler Joyner to continue representing the brand while putting on great classes. Looking ahead, we are going to focus heavily on growing our newer states while we also look for instructors and tourism partners in a few new cities. I still love teaching, but hope to spend most of this year teaching and training new instructors so I may temporarily step away from the classroom to continue refining our business model.

Heidi points out that it can be difficult to focus and refrain from going after too many new markets all at once, and that, despite her efforts, some of these markets are not quite ready to take off. To help curb this frustration, she has implemented a new mentality for herself: "I'm not going to push things if they aren't ready. I am always going to be proactive and will keep moving forward as fast as I can, but sometimes things cannot and *should not* be forced, and I'm learning to let things unfold more naturally." As legal cannabis consumption continues to spread across the country, Heidi Keyes will surely find the right way to spread her humor, joy, and creativity while continuing to foster understanding and acceptance within the marijuana movement.

———

Notes

1. Puff, Pass & Paint home page, last modified 2016, http://puffpassandpaint.com.

Diane Fornbacher

PUBLISHER OF *LADYBUD* MAGAZINE AND WEB SHOW

"I see myself as a vintage piece of this movement; I am still in circulation, but the industry needs some shiny new pennies to bring their value."

PUBLISHER OF *LADYBUD* magazine and the accompanying web show of the same name, Diane Fornbacher is a philosopher, artist, heroic activist, and mother who has brought all of her ferocity to the cannabis movement for the past two decades. She is a recipient of the NORML Pauline Sabin Award for her contributions to both grassroots organizations and national drug policy reform organizations and is a founding board member of many renowned cannabis associations. Diane is also a daring marijuana refugee whose commitment to promoting awareness, justice, and compassion for the cannabis movement is surpassed only by her devotion to her family. Her uncompromising, unabashed, and fearless efforts have improved the representation of women in cannabis media, a necessary endeavor on the path to gender equality.

Diane's fortitude is unquestionable. She suffers from Complex Post Traumatic Stress Disorder (CPTSD), a condition borne from a succession of traumatic circumstances Diane faced while growing up. In her childhood, Diane endured physical, psychological, and sexual abuse at the hands of her stepfather. Though Diane never told her mother about the abuse, her mother eventually discovered the truth for herself and, in a fit of rage, shot and killed her abusive husband before turning the gun on herself. After the deaths of her mother and stepfather, Diane moved from one ruthless environment to the next, moving in with with her father, whom she had not seen since she was six years old, and abusive stepmother. She ran away several times and was eventually placed in foster care. It wasn't until college that she discovered cannabis could effectively treat her CPTSD symptoms.

In 1996, Diane was arrested with "a pipe and a gram of weed" while she was an undergraduate at Pennsylvania State University's (PSU) satellite campus in Altoona which is, coincidentally, the birthplace and hometown of Harry Anslinger, the famed cannabis prohibitionist from the 1930s. Diane reveals, "I wasn't connected to the culture in any way until I got busted." Her court date was scheduled a month from her arrest, and needing a reason "to use this newfangled internet machine," she went back to the computer lab at PSU to search for information regarding her arrest and the state's marijuana laws. She discovered she was being charged under "The Controlled Substance, Drug, Device and Cosmetic Act" and that meant she was in serious trouble. While getting her fingerprints taken by local police, Diane remembers "the officer [saying], 'You don't look like the type that does *that* stuff.' I felt like they were throwing the book at me to make a point."

Diane was furious. By this time in her life, she was experiencing no benefit from traditional medications and says, "The only thing that worked to get me out of bed and into class was cannabis." She was outraged that her choice to medicate with an innocuous plant was complicated by outdated thinking and policy. Having gotten into PSU on partial scholarship, Diane met with the satellite campus' dean who she remembers saying, "We are not kicking you out of school, but we are asking you to leave and maybe apply again in a few years." Diane did not have any family she could move in with, so she "bounced around for a few months at various friends' houses" until she could find a more permanent situation that would allow her to be near the friends she had made during her freshman year. She finally found a sublet half a mile from the main campus of PSU. Determined to force a shift in the public understanding of marijuana, Diane entrenched herself in the movement, becoming an active reporter and protester. While Diane never returned to PSU for school, "I guess you could say I pursued my *life* education after getting busted alongside my friends who were still students."

Diane describes her entry into the world of cannabis as "sort of convoluted." It commenced when she started writing as a freelancer for a local magazine called *BUZZ*, based out of State College, Pennsylvania, and owned by Knight Ridder media company, a publisher that owned many newspapers east of the Mississippi in the late 1990s. She was promoted to the position of Poetry and Short Story Contest Judge and served as an Editor, as well as a Product and Show Review Critic covering the collegiate rock and roll scene. Diane remembers the publishers not being too keen on a piece she wrote about medical marijuana and expanding into alternative psychedelic therapies, and she was promptly fired. "So then,"

Diane declares, "I started getting arrested at protests that Dr. Julian Heicklen, Professor Emeritus of Chemistry, initiated at the PSU main gates." She was eventually hired by Heicklen to organize demonstrations, rallies, and press opportunities. This resulted in international coverage, which brought her to the attention of international cannabis magazine *High Times.* As a freelancer, she wrote for them periodically throughout the late 1990s and early 2000s when they were covering her activism and arrests or hiring her as a model.

Diane says she "technically" got involved in the movement in a formal sense when she, alongside several other women, founded the NORML Women's Alliance Foundation (NWAF). While starting NWAF, Diane discovered *SKUNK Magazine*, an international cannabis publication based out of Montreal, Canada, after "seeing *SKUNK*'s owner stand up for [her] against trolls in an online forum." Diane did some research and discovered that *SKUNK* had "no reasonably tangible website, no social media, [and] the majority of [its] pictures were objectifying women—which is not what we needed as an emerging industry." So she pulled no punches when responding to their eventual job offer: "I said, 'If you're reaching out to me for help, I'm gonna whip your asses into shape and I'm going to be very blunt with you: I'm not going to fuck around with this porn-like shit or stand by while women are presented this way.'" As an editor and, later, Managing Editor, her transformation of *SKUNK* grew their online following from about 100 to 100,000 people in the span of a year. She eventually left the magazine and made the decision to focus on traveling around the country promoting the NORML Women's Alliance. Diane was going to trade shows, becoming more aware of the industry, and remembers being disappointed by its representation: "Update your stock images—that's not what this industry is!" she roars, referring, once again, to images of women in scantily clad attire promoting "marijuana brands and dirty hands holding old-fashioned metal pipes."

While her career as a cannabis writer had taken off, Diane was still living in New Jersey, a state that did not allow her to consume her medicine of choice. So, in 2011, after a run in with Child Protective Services, Diane, her husband, and their two sons relocated to Colorado. Her voice full of frustration, she recounts:

> In 2011, my kids were in school and their drug education was comprised of outdated "Drug War Doctrines," so I was teaching them about the pros of hemp and marijuana at home. One day, my older son began talking about hemp at school as a viable solution to many of Earth's problems. The teachers asked him what hemp was and he said, "It's like marijuana but it doesn't get you high." They then cornered my son and interrogated him, in a violation of his rights—he is on the Autism spectrum, there are laws that protect kids from this type of thing—and they got out of my son that I "grew plants in the basement"—which were marigolds, by the way—and that got CPS sent to my house the same day we were trying to leave for my father's funeral. I am a philosopher, not a grower or a seller. In light of that, we hired a civil rights lawyer and got a letter back [from CPS] saying, "We have found that your charges are unfounded," but they had already traumatized my entire family. I realized—we are not safe here.

In New Jersey, PTSD is now a qualifying condition to receive medical marijuana, but it wasn't when they left the state. Diane understood that, to remain an activist and continue to treat her symptoms with cannabis, the family would have to relocate. After exploring a few places where Diane could safely use cannabis to treat her PTSD, they finally settled on Highlands Ranch, Colorado where Diane could access cannabis medicine legally. Colorado real estate was being snapped up quickly, so Diane knew they had to move fast. "We took two cars and a three-day trip to sign our mortgage." Diane did not want to leave her home, but like many other marijuana refugees, she did what she had to do to protect her family. Diane has maintained that her cannabis use helps her to be a better parent: "The fact that it helps me manage my PTSD symptoms makes me more present for my children." Even years after the fact, Diane's oldest son is still having a hard time working through their traumatic experience with CPS as well as the sadness of leaving his friends and family back home. But Diane is confident "he'll be ok" and foresees him potentially following in her footsteps: "He's very angry about the [War on Drugs]; he's watched a lot of videos about police interaction and I think it's turned him into an activist," she says with a smile.

Diane continued to thrive professionally upon relocating to Colorado. In 2012, she was unanimously voted in to serve on the board of NORML, and, in December of that year, her focus shifted to the alternative media platform, *Ladybud*. Disappointed by the content she saw propagated in the mainstream, Diane aspired to produce a thought-provoking, uncensored, and philosophical magazine that promoted culture, art, and empowerment.

> I wanted something that spoke to art as well as to the warrior spirit of the movement. I had worked for *SKUNK* and written for *High Times*, and I still didn't feel it was doing enough to change the perception of women in cannabis—I didn't see any sexually empowering articles or poetry and *Ladybud* was everything I felt mainstream media was missing. I wanted it to have barely any advertisements, like *Harper's Journal*—publishing mostly words, art, and poetry; where people could have a free voice to write about their cannabis use. . . . It was less censored than anything I've experienced, aside from the things I write personally.

Auspiciously, *Ladybud* was incorporated on 12/12/12, though the magazine did not debut until April 2013. For the first two years, Diane self-funded the publication from her savings, viewing it as "an investment in the future." She continues, "We didn't pay freelancers for the first few years—which they were okay with, as activists—and I would look at the calendar and find a solid schedule of eight to twelve articles per week." *Ladybud* has since expanded and now produces a companion web show which Diane says is much more manageable. "It's so much easier to do the show and get three months of content in an hour." She keeps the site running and maintains:

> Even though I'm behind on checking the spam, botting, the comments section, etc., I keep it live because we have several open-minded articles that track the trajectory of companies we are following. Some we admire, as well as a few who have taken advantage of patient families; it's important to know that story. [*Ladybud*] is very influential, even if we aren't rich. That often puts me at great odds with this industry. I hear stories about several companies bringing up in their board or executive meetings that, "If we piss off this person who owns *Ladybud*, it may seem like a small publication, but it will be bad for us."

Bad for them, indeed, because Diane is not shy about speaking up and speaking out when she sees injustice. Throughout her career, she has been approached by many media organizations "with money" who want to use her face and her voice to further their own agendas, but she is utterly disinterested by these offers. At *Ladybud*, she performs virtually *all* of the 10 to 15 roles that any traditional company requires in order to run smoothly, making her worth as an employee unquantifiable. More importantly, Diane hails from the activism community and refuses to involve herself with companies that lack integrity or do not give back to the marijuana movement.

"They don't speak to what I'm interested in. At *Ladybud*, we're 'classin' up the joint' [*Ladybud's* tagline], but we're also not," she laughs, and shares that she prefers "wearing flats—or no shoes—to wearing heels." Diane understands the business of activism, and the choice she wrestles with isn't what to wear so others will see her as the classy woman behind *Ladybud*. As someone who cares deeply about patient rights and advocacy while continuing to successfully run an online magazine, Diane has had a very hard time walking the fine line between taking advertising dollars from any one who will pay and maintaining the integrity of her publication.

Sometimes there are people who want to self-promote so they lie, dress it up, or "glitter-fy" their situation. They want to show their best face, their best story, but they have no integrity. I can hardly blame them, it's a byproduct of the selfie generation, but that's not my style. A lot of media is now disinclined to talk to me because I'm real with them. I won't even talk to a few publications anymore. . . . One of them called me up, told me, "We want to film you smoking a joint in front of your kids on a playdate," and I said, "I don't fucking think so—and you better not go to anyone else and ask them to do this. If anyone gets in trouble for this, I will make sure everyone knows [your publication was behind it]. If you fuck up, I'm going to call you out." The fever pitch of this industry does not move me in any way; I'm not so desperate for a story that I'm going to destroy lives. . . . Some of the companies and media approaching me [about partnering or advertising] are beneath me in that they lack intelligentsia, art, and philosophy.

Her indignation comes from an important place: she cares immensely about patients and families and is tired of seeing Big Business, or Big Media, take advantage of these people for corporate gain. She was breathing fire at this point, but Diane paused to reflect on her impact as a role model and mentor for many people in cannabis. She softens a bit, and humbly imparts some insightful wisdom:

I understand I've influenced a lot of people, but without the people before me and before them, none of us would be where we are. I'm glad to be at the top, on the side, to be an advisor behind the curtain. I'm trying to come to peace with where I've been and what I've done. Sometimes I'm proud of what I've done, but most of the time I'm just proud to be alive. My pride doesn't go to me; my pride goes to many others. When I look into the movement, [I] see Susan [Squibb], Christie [Lunsford], and—my biggest mentor—Debby Goldsberry, maintaining integrity through business. To put your heart on your sleeve and have it punched and get ripped off of you, that's when I'm proud. I'm proud when I see other people continuing. There are a lot of really great and redeeming people I have mentored and I felt like I didn't need my ego to tell me to stay involved when I needed to take care of myself. A lot of people, especially my own mentors, have become very close friends, but part of my personal growth has been understanding I need to be my own best friend. All of my work has culminated into a parallel of Diane growing at the same time I'm trying to grow this movement.

Diane says she is coming to peace with her place in the future of the marijuana movement. This past year, she bravely took a small step back from her work in order to better care for her health. On top of PTSD, Diane suffers from endometriosis, a painful disorder where tissue that normally lines the inside of the uterus, the endometrium, grows outside of the uterine wall. Associated pain from endometriosis can come and go, and for some women, including Diane, it can be absolutely debilitating. Her suffering is compounded as this pain is accompanied by Premenstrual Dysphoria, a hormone-induced depression which can trigger her Complex PTSD symptoms. Cannabis has been immensely helpful for her physical pain and mental anguish, but even with cannabis, Diane found it difficult to manage her business while experiencing chronic episodes throughout much of 2015. To her chagrin, she admits that she doesn't have the energy to continue to be involved in the same capacity that she once was. While she sighs, "I miss my bullhorn; I miss fighting on the front lines," she concedes, "that's not my priority anymore." She has already sacrificed so much to carve a clearer path for others to make their entry into the cannabis industry, and she is welcoming of newcomers, as long as they act with integrity. "I see myself as a vintage piece of this movement; I am still in circulation, but the industry needs some shiny new pennies to bring their value." Diane offers counsel to "new pennies" attempting to follow in her footsteps:

My advice is this: It's rock and roll. It's a nascent industry and the [War on Drugs] is not over. Know your history and your civil liberties. Know what you're getting yourself into. The more active you are, the more it finds you. That's what it boils down to; cannabis is a microcosm of a macro world; we are a reflection of the world. I tell people to not close themselves off, to act local, be local, to look within themselves. It's time for you to ask yourself where you can go right, as it relates to yourself.

Diane has given so much more to the movement than she has received in return. For much of her life, she has had every reason to quit and fall victim to despair, yet, astonishingly, she's persevered. She puts the "grit" in "integrity." For the first time in her interview, she falters for a moment, confessing, "This [movement] has taken everything from me—I've never made more than I've spent on this. I've never paid myself." She pauses, then recovering, chuckles, "Once I used my *Ladybud* card to rent a car, but I fucked it up and still wound up paying out of pocket! With all that's been said, I'm proud of [those who have worked alongside of me] and I'm glad I have my family with me." And it is clear that there are so many in the industry who feel proud, humbled, honored, and grateful to have fought on the front lines of cannabis with Diane Fornbacher.

Maureen McNamara

FOUNDER AND CHIEF FACILITATOR OF CANNABIS TRAINERS

"Declare it. Create it. And just start doing your work."

"I DON'T THINK of myself as a *female* business owner or a *female* entrepreneur. I am a business owner and an entrepreneur—who is also a woman." Maureen McNamara is a quick-thinking go-getter and self-described dreamer who loves to empower others and to laugh (a lot). With more than 20 years of experience as a professional trainer, she has trained and certified over 10 thousand employees, managers, and owners in national certification programs for small, locally-owned businesses as well as international corporations. In 2014, she founded Cannabis Trainers through which, as Chief Facilitator and Founder, she has worked with thousands of cannabis industry professionals.

Maureen's path to carving out her niche in cannabis humbly begins where many recent college grads cut their teeth in the real world: waiting tables and serving drinks. She jokes, "I graduated with a philosophy degree and a French minor, so, therefore, I began bartending and working in restaurants!" Being that she actually enjoyed the job and displayed exemplary work ethic, Maureen started to rapidly progress, and was soon training new employees. She says, "At first, I thought it would be a 'for now' job, but I was good at it, and I grew in the training space within the hospitality industry." As a trainer, Maureen quickly worked her way up the ranks, and, before long, was facilitating training workshops at a corporate level for grand openings of new restaurants. In 1998, she left her corporate gig and started working for herself leading food safety classes and hospitality trainings.

The idea to go into cannabis first occurred to Maureen in November 2013.

I was teaching probably my one hundredth-something food safety class. I had been leading food safety training classes for nearly 20 years at this point, and before every class I always work the room, talk to people, and try to get a feel for what people do and at which restaurants and hotels. I'll never forget this one woman in the third row, right side of the room. She was very quiet and avoided my pre-class questions. She was being very discreet and then finally said something I didn't understand. I asked her to repeat herself and she burst out excitedly, "Pot brownies! I make pot brownies!" A lightbulb went off—I was thrilled that people making infused products were committed to doing it with excellence. I remember that "ding" moment—when I realized this was what I needed to do.

In January 2014, with Colorado just two months away from recreational legalization, Maureen began brewing her professional idea.

In her wisdom gleaned from decades of experience certifying people in food safety and responsible alcohol service for the hospitality industry, Maureen saw that she could translate her expertise in training and professional service development and customize a program to fit the needs of the cannabis industry. She muses, "The transition was relatively easy, in hindsight." Tailoring her skills and customizing her offerings may have been "relatively easy" for Maureen, but she admits she still had some initial hesitation about associating her business with such a "taboo" industry. She found herself worrying from time to time about what people would think, but says she quickly got over the hesitation when she realized: "Who cares?! I figured legalization is happening—whether people are prohibitionists or in full support of it, it's happening. I'm here providing my services to make sure it happens with integrity and compliance."

Maureen shares that her mother did "raise her eyebrows" at first when she told her she would be training people to sell pot. She also remembers her father "paused for five seconds and then said, 'Great idea, honey, very good idea!'" Her mother did not take long to come around, and Maureen acknowledges that having this family support "definitely made things a lot easier." Today, Maureen's mother is currently healing from lung cancer, and it seems to bring Maureen a sense of peace that she is able to have conversations with her mom about cannabis. She says her mother has recently become "more open to the idea of cannabis being a contribution to her healing, more so than she would have been three years ago when I first had this [business] idea."

Like her parents, Maureen's existing clients were also surprisingly supportive of her new venture. To this day, she has not given up any part of her other businesses and continues to lead food and alcohol safety trainings while also working as a professional life coach. She appreciates her hospitality related business because of its longevity. At this point in her career, she says she has fallen into the "ease" of it: "I just have clients who call and request classes, and I do outsource some of these classes now. I have absolutely directed the majority of my energy and time, intention and attention, to nurturing Cannabis Trainers."

The support and receptiveness of her clients and parents remains a bright spot in Maureen's story. Another highlight occurred during the very first cannabis-focused food class Maureen taught. "NPR was there, the media, the room was packed, everything *sold out*. It was a very exciting launch to this endeavor. I had people calling from around the country who I had never spoken to," she beams. Maureen also recounts her "tear inducing laughter" after being photobombed by Melissa Etheridge backstage at the Women Grow Leadership Summit in 2016. Still, of all the wonderful parts of her career, the thing Maureen cherishes the most is the feeling she gets after teaching, especially when patient specialists or budtenders come up to thank her. "Those small, sweet moments are extraordinary highlights for me."

Maureen chuckles as she confesses, "I have had a pretty easy ride—but it has still been a rollercoaster." Her metaphor alludes to the fact that, though her experience in cannabis has had its fair amount of ups, Maureen's journey has not been without its downs, twists, turns and loops. A constant frustration is that "it's so slow"; she feels it often takes much longer than expected for her to get through all the "red tape" when launching her projects. During tough times, Maureen says she relies on her background in coaching to power her through. "I am interesting because I am a trained life coach, meaning I can provide insight when my clients are questioning themselves or becoming worried during the periods of struggle. I often use some of my own tools on myself and it helps to make things better and easier for me." Maureen recalls, "I remember in the first half of 2014, although I had my other businesses, 85% of my energy and focus was on Cannabis Trainers. There was such a steep learning curve for me at that time. To learn cannabis, speak cannabis, and understand this plant." She remembers how draining the process felt and had to suppress the lurking doubt that she would ever get her idea off and running in the way she had planned.

Despite the successful launch of her program, registration in the classes that followed was shockingly low, to Maureen's disappointment and disbelief. She recounts one such class that had only two people enroll, and remembers thinking, "I can't build a national business when only two people show up." She even considered cancelling the class. But Maureen decided to go ahead, refusing to abandon her students despite the meager number of participants. To her surprise, she had a "delightful" class with the two gentlemen in attendance. One of those first two students remains a client of Maureen's to this day, and the other she anticipates working with in the future. Maureen says that, during the early days of Cannabis Trainers, regardless of how hard she worked, she often questioned: "Am I doing enough, quickly enough?" She warns that those limiting voices can often "derail" entrepreneurs and adds, "Not allowing those voices to detract from the overall goal or lure us off track is really important."

The ups and downs of the cannabis industry, coupled with the stigma surrounding those who work within it, has undoubtedly resulted in many people shying away from diving in head first. Maureen views this hesitation from others as an advantage, as this reluctance has led to "a unique place where an emerging market is available for us." She agrees that, whereas other booming industries like investment banking and technology were dominated by large corporate entities—and men—from the early stages of their growth, cannabis has deterred most of those same entities due to its controversiality and volatile nature. That initial stalling, Maureen believes, has resulted in greater opportunity for savvy entrepreneurs, and she is all for it. "When I see an open field of opportunity, like we have in the cannabis industry, it thrills me for anyone to bring their talent to this game. As a founding member of Women

Grow, I am especially enthusiastic to invite women to bring their talents and energies to this industry." She further urges "for anyone, whatever your talent or special contribution is, [to] *get off the sidelines.* Come join this industry. The more people who can bring their energy to it, the more it will flourish."

Maureen also has a unique opinion on whether women in cannabis are in a particularly advantageous position to break through the grass ceiling. She is "thrilled" by her observation that female leadership in cannabis seems to be more common than in other industries, but, she continues, "my bottom line is this: I think in this industry we need to move beyond the illusion of a glass ceiling; what if it doesn't exist at all? Right now we are building the structure, so we don't need to box ourselves in. The walls, the containment, the ceilings—*it's all an illusion.* We can make this space as expansive as we choose." Maureen believes men and women alike are responsible for encouraging businesses to transcend the abstract barriers and limitations and work toward a more inclusive culture overall. "I think when businesses grow and expand, keeping the culture [of inclusion] alive is up to everybody. When we see or experience things that defy that culture, or would negatively impact it, it's up to all of us to speak up in such a way as to demand or encourage a shift."

To the women considering a shift into the marijuana business, Maureen offers a few words of transcendent wisdom through relating an experience from her early days as an entrepreneur.

I remember very clearly in late 1998 when I quit my job to be self-employed—which felt more like unemployed—I had been to a conference and I saw a woman who was traveling internationally and putting on workshops all around the world. I was in awe of her. I wanted to speak to her, so I finally worked up enough courage and approached her [to ask for advice]. She looked at me, paused, and said, *"Just start doing your work."* Those five words resonated with me so powerfully and really struck a chord with me. I would give similar advice to women desiring a change in careers or curious about this industry. *Declare it, create it, and just start doing your work.*

That is the mantra to which Maureen credits a great deal of her success as an entrepreneur both within and outside of cannabis. "I get ideas, I get inspired, and I create them. I think this goes beyond the cannabis industry."

Maureen says her work in this "fascinating industry" is far from over. Cannabis Trainers is growing its team of facilitators who lead the program in different parts of the country, from coast to coast. Looking ahead, though she actively encourages newcomers to the space, she won't be stepping aside anytime soon. "My primary focus is education. That will continue to be my team's primary contribution. I've been running my classes very old school, so our endeavor moving forward is to transform our Sell-SMaRT™ program by adding an e-learning or a blended e-learning series." When that is accomplished, Maureen hopes she can expand the reach of her program globally to other emerging cannabis markets. While she is unable to divulge specific details (yet), Maureen also has some exciting collaborative endeavors that will be unveiled in the coming months and beyond.

Additionally, Maureen declares her mission for Cannabis Trainers is to keep holding the industry, and those operating within it, to the highest standard.

> My vision for the future is that, as cannabis continues to be sold medically and for adult use in many more places around the country and the world, we are here to ensure it happens compliantly, with professionalism, and with the utmost integrity. We want to make sure every cultivator, extractor, and dispensary has the opportunity to stay open in order to provide safe access to cannabis.

She firmly believes that "having a well trained team, inspired to play by the rules, allows that to happen with greater ease." Maureen McNamara balances her high expectations and her demand for professionalism with her unrelenting idealism and her joyful spirit. Wishfully, she also describes a more personal and playful dream for the future: "To live in a world where laughter is the elixir of choice, caramel flavored kisses are readily available, and judgment is as out of style as the rotary phone."

Giadha Aguirre de Carcer

FOUNDER AND CEO OF NEW FRONTIER DATA

"I believe we can absolutely teach new women what we have learned and where the pitfalls lie."

"WHAT DOES IT take for an educated, professional woman to succeed in business *and* in love?" This was a question Giadha Aguirre de Carcer had struggled with for ages. A serial entrepreneur, Giadha has a long history of being married—to her work; something that her significant others had not always understood or accepted. "I was in a relationship for some time when my boyfriend at the time dropped an ultimatum on me," she recalls. "He said I worked too much and that I had to choose between my career and him," a choice men are not often faced with and an ultimatum most men are never issued. "I don't react well to ultimatums so it really wasn't a tough decision for me!" With her love life now nonexistent, Giadha turned her full attention to her work. At the time, she was running a successful consulting company that worked with businesses interested in moving into emerging markets around the world including South America, China, and Russia.

This was Giadha's third company, GNI International; she had already launched and operated two other data-driven businesses. Prior to these endeavors, she was a successful investment banker working with JPMorgan Chase in both their Manhattan and London offices and was the co-founder and COO of Florida-based First Federal Transportation. Giadha also spent time in the defense, technology, and telecommunications sectors and describes herself as an expert in emerging, high growth markets.

While business was certainly good, Giadha recognized early on that a consulting business would be difficult to "scale" or grow to meet expanding demand. She was eager to do something bigger that would give her the opportunity for a lucrative exit plan and, as a newly single woman approaching 40, still wanted to find the answer to her question: *can a woman succeed in business and in love?* She decided that this was her time to do something she describes as "quirky and crazy." She launched a Kickstarter campaign to finance the making of a documentary about herself pursuing both love and entrepreneurship over a 90 day period. Her campaign's $35,000 goal was funded within 72 hours, primarily backed by professional women seeking answers to the same question. "I hired someone to follow me around for 90 days. I tried all forms of dating: consulting a matchmaker, OKCupid, speed dating, dating apps, etc., and allowed the entire process to be filmed. Additionally, my commitment was to launch a business within the same 90 days. I wanted to figure out the formula for women who truly want both love and a high powered career. I wanted to have an answer to the question at the end of 90 days."

As soon as the campaign was funded, Giadha set out to find a cinematographer. A close friend also joined the project as Giadha's mentor. With the documentary logistics coming together, Giadha had to make the next big decision:

> What business should I launch? . . . At this time, cannabis was not on my radar. I was actively transitioning out of my consulting firm when I received a call from a group in Maryland that was familiar with our firm's capabilities on the research and analytics side and wanted to hire my firm to evaluate the cannabis landscape and opportunities. As I do with all new engagements, I immediately began looking for industry data and reports. To my surprise, there was basically nothing available. Given my background in emerging markets, data, and industry analytics, it hit me. That was it. The lightbulb went on and New Frontier Data was born.

New Frontier Data was built over the course of Giadha's 90-day project and formally launched in August 2014. While Giadha did not find permanent love throughout the process, her takeaways were shared with all funders. "I learned a lot. When you're a career driven woman it is very hard to separate love and business."

Aside from the challenges of managing a documentary, the dating circuit, and a new company, Giadha was also met with a great deal of criticism from people ranging from family members to the media. "Someone referred to the documentary as public masturbation," she recalls, "while others told me it was obscene and I was embarrassing myself." Giadha notes that, while she went on a number of filmed dates, she always had a chaperone, never even kissed any of her dates, and was surprised that some felt she was "slutterizing herself" on camera. "My mom was not supportive at all. And when I chose cannabis as the business topic, it made it even worse." While Giadha did not express fearfulness surrounding the industry or the risks associated with it, she did worry about her reputation as well as the reputation of her family, explaining that she was much more "concerned about the public stigma than about the federal regulatory system." For more than seven years, she had been assessing risk in emerging markets where "regulatory systems are often sub-optimal to say the least. . . . I was comfortable knowing there was always a way and a path. I was less comfortable when I thought about potential damage this could cause to my hard earned reputation and to my family."

As an immigrant born in Italy then raised in France and Spain, Giadha went through four years of community college before enrolling at a four-year institution. She went on to complete her undergraduate degree from the University of Pennsylvania, an achievement of which her family was incredibly proud, then earned her MA from Georgetown University. "I remember my mom worrying that I was ruining all of this hard work by going into cannabis, and that people would think that we were a drug cartel because of my involvement in the industry and because we are Hispanic." Friends and colleagues reacted differently to the project. Some were supportive and deeply interested in her work, while others disassociated themselves from her in person and by unfriending her on Facebook, unlinking her on LinkedIn, and sharing their concerns about her decision.

> There were times where I wondered what I would do if my decision to work in cannabis did not pan out. I knew I was putting myself at risk. I knew I wouldn't be rehired by government agencies I had previously worked with, and was not confident I would be hired back easily by a bank. But I had reached a point where I just didn't care. I decided I was going to go balls to the wall; the level of frustration I had at that point was intense—I [was] gonna do something a little nutty. I was tired of all of the bullshit and I was ready and willing to take on a greater risk for a greater reward.

Fortunately for the industry, Giadha forged ahead, growing New Frontier Data into over a 20 person team based out of Washington, DC. Many of her former colleagues who once questioned her judgment have since reappeared looking for opportunities with her or within the industry at large. "I think when people saw me included in reputable reporting on CNN and the like, they realized that I was legitimate and was doing something serious."

As a female founder and CEO of companies inside and outside the cannabis industry, Giadha possesses a unique perspective when it comes to the glass ceiling, or grass ceiling, in the case of cannabis, and how easily—or not—a woman can climb the ranks.

> I would say, for me, that the experience has been much better in cannabis than anywhere else. When I was working in the government and technology space, as a comparison, there seemed to be a pre-existing boys club with a profile requirement to enter: white, male, older. This industry was born from a movement, a very diverse movement, without pre-existing anything, and I think that made a difference.

In the banking world, Giadha worked with many men and a handful of women. "Oftentimes, women in banking were not eager to help [other] women climb the ladders. They paid their dues and they wanted to see to it that you pay your dues, too. Many women did not seem interested in making it easier for new women coming into the profession—something I found to be the complete opposite in cannabis."

Her journey through the industry has not always been easy. Giadha remembers initially being exiled for being a "suit," coming to cannabis from a banking background. She recalls men and women from the activist community specifically being fairly closed off to her, questioning her intentions and reasons behind getting involved. She also had her fair share of problems with several "shady characters" that she encountered.

Most of my low points in this industry have stemmed from people—this industry is very complex and colorful, which can be good, bad, and ugly. It's good because it's diverse in terms of ideology; colorful because the industry is liberal, accepting, and highly intellectually stimulating. But it [can be challenging] because there are certainly characters that were very questionable, from investors to employees to consultants. . . . Especially in the beginning, it was very difficult to separate the good from the bad. And given the greyness of our industry, it makes sense that the industry was attracting people like this.

Giadha admits she was taken advantage of when she was new, as she felt the warmth of the cannabis community and let her guard down. While that time period was a struggle, she came out on top with many lessons learned, one of the greatest being that finding and retaining the right people and the best talent is the key to being successful in this sometimes tumultuous industry.

Fortunately, Giadha made some exceptional connections early in her career with well regarded companies, such as The ArcView Investment Group, and by finding strong female peers to lean on and learn from, such as Kristin Fox, Editor in Chief of Marijuana Investor News and a founding board member of 100 Women in Hedge Funds. "[Kristin] saw that I was hungry and she literally held my hand through the process." Giadha also remembers connecting with other women along the way who were in a similar position to her, trying to navigate the industry and find a niche opportunity. "There was instant camaraderie when I met women like that. We shared an instant bond as we were both facing the unknown." While Giadha's darker moments in cannabis stemmed from people who did not have her best interests in mind, her highlights also stemmed from people. "It's interesting to me that my best and worst moments were both driven by the same variable."

As New Frontier Data enters into its third year in business, the company continues to grow and is looking for professionals in their second office to be based out of Denver. She describes her team as highly driven and passionate, and feels similarly about her "equally driven partners and investors." "I have never seen a more cohesive group of people with one focused goal."

Due to the great support she received in 2014, Giadha is committed to "paying it forward" as it relates to mentoring and supporting women who are interested in coming into the cannabis industry. "I think it's time for us to help others. While we haven't figured it all out yet and we still have a massive road ahead, I believe we can absolutely teach new women what we have learned and where the pitfalls lie. One piece of advice I would offer to women is to 'give it to get it.' If you offer to help others or volunteer time, people will see that and they'll be even more inclined to support you in return." Giadha has an extensive track record of supporting her fellow female entrepreneurs. At one time she ran the Women Entrepreneurship Reinforcement program in support of female entrepreneurs nationwide, and was also the Executive Director of the Grassroots Innovation Network, a nonprofit organization focused on funding college students' business ideas globally.

Giadha Aguirre de Carcer has no plans to rest anytime soon. "[New Frontier Data] is my unicorn. There is nothing I love more than coming into the office everyday and continuing to build. The next three years will be extremely exciting for us. I am focused on a double bottom line. I am a businesswoman so, yes, making money and capitalizing is important, but I also have a heart and I want to be part of something that gratifies my business' bottom line and my heart's bottom line—I never want this experience to end." While some of New Frontier Data's plans are off-the-record (for now), Giadha shared that the company is forging some massive relationships outside of the cannabis sphere to elevate what the industry is doing now. These partnerships will help New Frontier Data continue to grow both domestically and internationally. "Having partnerships outside of cannabis proves that the stigma is changing. And I am pleased that our company can open some of these doors while providing quality, agnostic, real time business intelligence." New Frontier Data's wholesome approach to the industry, driven forward by Giadha's hand-picked team of professionals, is bound to bring new intel to this rapidly growing industry. "We intend to shine light on the issues, even if they're the ones the industry doesn't want us to share. We might piss people off, but that's okay. It's for the greater good and will help all of us move forward."

———

Karson Humiston

FOUNDER AND PRESIDENT OF VANGST TALENT

"Stay humble—
a few successes doesn't warrant a celebration—you need
to stay attentive, grounded, and nimble."

BREAKING THE GRASS ceiling is neither a one person job nor a job that belongs solely to women. Few exemplify that sentiment of leadership better than Karson Humiston who, as Founder and President of Vangst Talent, is not only working alongside other cannabis pioneers—both men and women—to break the grass ceiling, but creating a space within the industry where other women can follow suit. At just 24 years old, Karson is a tenacious maverick at the top of her game and possesses wisdom well beyond her years.

Karson joined the cannabis space in 2015 during her final semester at St. Lawrence College in Canton, NY. At that time, Karson had just sold her first company, On Track Adventures, a business she started in college that helped students coordinate adventurous trips for their school breaks. She managed recruiters and Student Trip Leaders all over the east coast who worked under her to arrange trips and market them on their respective campuses. While, at a first glance, this experience may not seem directly related to Karson's career path in cannabis, she applied the lessons she learned in her first business venture and dove fearlessly into this new industry; by her second year of operation, she has achieved significant success.

Karson recalls the stress of managing recruiters and staff, learning how to start—and manage—a new company, all while navigating her college courses. When she decided to sell On Track Adventures, Karson knew she wouldn't be fulfilled unless she started something else.

> I remember asking myself what I would do with the rest of my life. My parents were asking, their friends were asking, my teachers were asking; everyone was encouraging me to take a job and choose a career path. My parents never quit reminding me that the real world was approaching, and I felt a lot of pressure to make some decisions.

Karson struggled with the job search process, the same way many college seniors do as they try to weigh their personal goals and interests against jobs that pay well and offer attractive credentials.

> I spent a lot of time thinking about how hard it was, as a recent college graduate, to find a job, and even more, how difficult it was to find a *cool* job. I came to realize that I had a sizeable network of college students because of my former company, and decided that my next business should be oriented around helping these students find positions.

Although she makes it sound simple, Karson's idea would develop into something that was completely new to the sphere of recruitment.

Karson spent the final months of the semester heading to various tradeshows, and eventually found herself at a cannabis business exposition. "I had business cards printed with Gradujuana on them and decided to walk around this trade show promoting my business concept as though it was already alive and operational. I started by asking people if they wanted interns or recent college grads to support their cannabis businesses that upcoming summer [2015]. The response was overwhelmingly positive so I went back to school, hopped on a library computer, and built the Gradujuana website." She proclaims, laughing, "It sucked!" Still, this action was an important stepping stone for Karson because she "made two key decisions right then and there: I decided to charge $500 per intern and also decided to move to Colorado immediately following graduation to explore what my mom was referring to as the 'weed hiring business.'" Her decision was met with equal parts enthusiasm and dismay. "I remember some of our family friends saying that I was going to ruin my reputation by working in the industry. Others made comments that I could wind up in jail, or that I had so much potential in life and that going into this industry was insane." Fortunately, Karson's parents have always supported her, especially her father, a serial entrepreneur in his own right. "I don't mean to rip on these people for being cautious and looking out for me—it came from a good place—but I knew I was going to do this and [the decision] felt right."

Karson wasted no time planning her move to Colorado. She describes how it was a complete whirlwind: graduating college, moving home, organizing her possessions, repacking the car, and driving to Colorado all in roughly a week's time. And, upon arrival, she got straight to work promoting her intern service by going door-to-door within the industry. In August 2015, Karson, who was still operating as a one-woman show, approached Jay and Diane Czarkowski of Canna Advisors to see if she could find them some summer interns. To Karson's surprise, the duo ended up asking her if she and her team were able to support full-time staffing and hiring needs. Rather than admitting that she was still working by herself and had not yet considered taking on this level of work, Karson remembers thinking on her feet and telling them that she could absolutely handle it. Before she walked out of their office, Karson had a contract to fill three full-time roles for Canna Advisors—and a brand new business idea. She successfully completed her hiring assignment and, soon after, transformed Gradujuana into her current company, Vangst Talent, a full-fledged staffing and recruitment company dedicated to the cannabis industry. "When I filled those three roles, I realized that this was going to work. I had a proof of concept, a little bit of money in the bank, and decided to take a risk by hiring my first employee, Jordan [Smith]. While I was new to recruitment and hadn't done executive level staffing before this engagement with the Czarkowskis, I worked hard and got it done."

Jordan, who still works closely with Karson at Vangst, has also been a huge source of support for Karson, their many clients, and their rapidly growing team. "Hiring the right people is so critical," says Karson, who, at the time of publishing, now employs 15 full-time recruiters and account managers—primarily women—with clientele nationwide.

While things came together for Karson relatively quickly, there was still plenty of time for challenges to arise. Karson describes being 23 years old and navigating cash flow crunches and the struggles that come from reinvesting all profits back into a business. "There were times when I wasn't sure how I'd make payroll a week out! I was extremely risky early on, investing practically everything I earned back into the business. I never took investment from anyone so this is my company entirely—for better or for worse! There were absolutely times where I wondered if I was in way over my head."

As a young female, Karson faces unique struggles beyond financial strife. Managing people twice her age presented a very specific set of challenges. Early on Karson "hired a guy who was much older than I was, with the hope that he would come in and knock it out of the park because of his many years of experience. It ended up not being a good fit, in part because he seemed much more interested in trying to run the company than do the job he was hired to do." In addition to navigating relationships with her own personnel, Karson has also been targeted by dozens of people, both men and women, who reach out to her sharing unsolicited observations and advice.

While Karson credits several well-intentioned men and women for helping guide and coach her, she was frustrated by the number of people who felt that she needed to take their advice simply because of her young age.

I think young entrepreneurs need to be cautious when taking advice. Take all advice, especially from those older than you, with a grain of salt. I had so many people tell me I wouldn't be able to do this on my own and that I should give them a percentage of my business so they could oversee me and make sure I was operating correctly. People who want to partner up, and people who truly believed that they deserved a piece of my business simply because they had more years on this earth. I didn't take any of these deals and I am fortunate that I didn't because, while I was definitely hungry for advice back then, I also wanted to be patient in assessing possible partners and mentors.

Karson has, on her own terms, found several mentors in this industry, and enjoys the opportunity to brainstorm with and learn from them. While she exudes a palpable confidence and pride in her accomplishments, Karson is also respectful and incredibly down to earth. Her voice softens as she mentions a few women who have had a strong influence in her career. "Di [Czarkowski] literally helped me to change my entire business model and has become a friend of mine who I truly look up to. Many of my clients have also become friends and partners of mine, watching out for me, and teaching me everyday. Jaime Lewis, a client-turned-friend, Halston Puchek of Wurk . . ." Her voice trails off as the list continues—when she stops, it feels like a moment of humble reflection and appreciation.

Each month, Karson works with hundreds of interested candidates hoping to work in this extremely competitive industry, and has probably heard from just as many entrepreneurs seeking her guidance as they consider how to best enter this market. Her advice is simple and candid: "Have confidence in yourself and in your idea and never, ever give up. Yeah, you'll probably pivot, make changes, and change course, but once you get going, don't stop or turn back. I spend a lot of time reading about successful entrepreneurs and I can tell you this: the successful ones are the ones who get knocked down a thousand times and still keep getting up." She also advises that when you're brainstorming or sitting down with people to share your ideas, have them sign a non-disclosure agreement. "Never give up more [information] than you need to. And stay humble. A few successes doesn't warrant a celebration; you need to stay attentive, grounded, and nimble."

Speaking to those who are looking for a foot in the door is what gets Karson out of bed each day. "There is nothing better than hearing from candidates who we have placed who are so, so excited about their new role, their new company, and the industry as a whole. So many of these people turn around and encourage others to find their dream job by reaching out to our team at Vangst. This makes me so happy. I want to pay it forward and help candidates, especially women, find a place in this industry." Her strength and tenacity benefit everyone working in cannabis as Karson continues to help raise the industry's bar by drawing top talent from other channels like high tech, law, and science. "This industry is super challenging; everyday there are new hurdles, especially for women. But, overall, I think this industry is welcoming and accommodating towards women and I am so happy that Vangst has played a part in helping women land their dream jobs."

Karson's commitment to the advancement of women in this space is obvious, but she stresses that cultivating female talent in cannabis is not a job only women should tackle.

Men are a big part of the process and a big part of my process. One of my closest friends and industry colleagues, Ryan Smith of LeafLink, has been an incredible source of support for me professionally—largely because he never treats me differently than he would a male peer. He sees my strengths and views me as an equal. I am also incredibly fortunate to have a father who has supported me and my vision for this since the start. I know men like this are not a dime a dozen, so I am very grateful, and think it is important for women to find strong men, as well as women, to have in their corner.

Karson Humiston is relentless. She takes her work and her role in this industry seriously, but maintains a great sense of humor, something that helps her shake off the rough days and power through the unexpected pitfalls. This attitude will continue to serve her well as Vangst keeps building and shaping the industry, full steam ahead. "Vangst is going to keep charging forward. We are filling jobs throughout the country, in many markets, and are drawing top talent from everywhere. Through this process, I hope that Vangst can continue to play a significant part in elevating the industry." What Karson lacks in years, she makes up for—many times over—in gusto. Her accomplishments at such a young age, in such a short period of time, are truly astounding. As the future of women in weed unfolds, she is surely someone to watch on her path to crashing through the grass ceiling and repainting the picture of a leading player at the top of a multibillion dollar industry.

Afterword

THE RUNNING JOKE is that, because I went to university for musical theatre, I spent four years (and exorbitant amounts of money) learning how to
properly roll around on the floor and *breathe*. While, *yes*, I did take voice
and movement classes and, *true*, those exercises were a large part of my
class time, I learned so much more—most of which I was not able to fully
internalize as a student. It has taken me years since graduating to truly
appreciate the value of one of the most important lessons: actors are storytellers and the greatest storytellers are also the greatest empaths. It takes
vulnerability and courage to enter the life of a character and fully live that
character's story on stage. If the performance is good, the audience can
experience the fear, hurt, rage, excitement, joy, and catharsis of another
human being from the safe physical and emotional distance of their seat
in the theatre.

I no longer perform on stage, but I still love to tell stories. This
book serves as a written extension of my empathy for the human
condition—specifically, as an extension of my empathy for women. As
a woman, I feel empathy for other professional women because, like
seemingly every other major industry, showbiz is dominated by men.
While the theatre can be a wonderfully embracing and diverse place,
women and minorities still face the same hurdles as they do in other industries. I personally endured and witnessed others cope with chauvin-
ism, misogyny, and male entitlement during my time in professional
theatre, and rarely spoke up about it out of fear that I would damage my
reputation and hurt my career. In my mid-twenties, I began thinking
about a new career path for myself and made the difficult decision to

walk away from the world of acting and performance. While I started working full-time for a corporate company, I also found myself drawn to the cannabis industry and became curious about its opportunities. My interest stemmed from two places: a love of marijuana and the buzz that cannabis was welcoming smart, career-driven women to lead its massive growth.

When I first approached my childhood friend, Ashley Picillo, and asked her to help me get my foot in the cannabis door, she immediately embraced me. I felt validated and confident that I had made a wise decision; I was finally working in an environment where being a woman had more advantages than disadvantages. Ashley shared that she had developed a panel for the March 2017 SXSW Conference; she called it *Breaking the Grass Ceiling* and was considering putting together an accompanying book. Intrigued, I encouraged her to step on the gas so this piece could launch at the event—within a few hours, we got to work. I eagerly anticipated interviewing 21 women who had crashed past their male peers to break through the glass ceiling, creating the first multibillion dollar industry that was *not* dominated by men. I planned to retell their stories in a form that would encourage fellow women—like *me*—to join us in this new industry. I was excited to share these stories with newcomers, like myself, so they could emulate these women and their various pathways to the top. To my considerable surprise, what I thought we would write and the book we ultimately put together were very different.

Soon after beginning our interview process, I realized that women in cannabis face many of the same boundaries that women encounter in other industries as they strive to be heard in a man's world. So I took a step back and concluded that this was not going to be a book about women who had already broken the ceiling, but rather about those who are *actively breaking it*—present tense. It is imperative that their stories be gathered and told so that others can learn from what these women have already endured. I knew my background in theatre had prepared me to do this.

In acting school, after watching a performance, we were usually asked: what did you learn? When I asked myself that question after writing this book, I had several important answers. First, I learned that these women share a common thread in that they all care—deeply. They care for their children and families, for their friends and colleagues, for each other, for the world, and for people they have yet to meet. They care so much that they have risked, sacrificed, and kept going—even when things were at their bleakest—soldiering on in their fight for what is right. Second, the stories of these amazing, pioneering women revealed to me that they all are actively working to *break the grass ceiling* in two ways. The most obvious way is that they are fighting and struggling on their climb up to that ceiling so they can burst through it themselves. The other way is harder to observe; it's more subtle, but, arguably, more impactful. These women are supporting each other and recruiting male allies to develop this industry into one without a ceiling at all.

Through this process, I have surmised that, in order for women to achieve parity on all levels, we all need to move beyond the assumption that our potential as a gender can be limited or capped by a ceiling. We can do that either by working so hard to reach the seemingly immeasurable height, *or* we can break it in the sense that we cease to acknowledge its existence at all. Through empathy and storytelling, we—men and women alike—can learn, adjust, and evolve by constructing a new and better environment. We can care for each other and help each other, working together to make the cannabis industry a limitless place, one that is welcoming to all, encouraging to all, and supportive of all. This industry can be a microcosm that preserves and fosters diversity and defends those who can't defend themselves when someone threatens this cohesive mentality. So many fierce, successful women coming together to contribute to this collection serves as proof that the latter is possible. Because cannabis is still a nascent industry, we have the power to build it from the ground up, and it is vitally important that we all work together to fashion it in such a way that the history of suppression in other industries is not repeated here. If we can do that, we can lead by example and encourage other industries to follow suit, thus rewriting the rules of how women operate in the business world at large.

When I was acting and my character choices felt stale or tired, it was usually because I was making assumptions about the character. In those situations I learned to ask: what if the opposite were true? When my assumptions about this book were proven false, I asked: what is the opposite of breaking the grass ceiling? The answer certainly isn't fixing it, but rather to transcend the very idea of it. What if it didn't exist at all?

—Lauren Devine

About the Author

ASHLEY PICILLO WAS born and raised in Massachusetts and holds a BS in Business Administration from Northeastern University in Boston. She has had a lifelong passion for developing business ideas and was certain she would start and end her career wearing stilettos and blazers in New York City. At 22 years old, Ashley had two major wake up calls: Wall Street was the absolute wrong environment for her creativity and entrepreneurship to flourish, and—while plans and logistics are important—*they are also flexible and meant to be changed.* With little warning to friends and family, Ashley headed to Hawaii as part of Teach For America, where she went on to teach in a low-income school on the North Shore of O'ahu. While working in a classroom, Ashley recognized her deep love for teaching and educating and concurrently pursued a Master of Arts degree in Teaching from Chaminade University in Honolulu, Hawaii.

In January 2014, Ashley moved back to NYC and began looking for Operations positions within education. She was hired by a company based in NYC, for a role scheduled to start in June 2014. With a few months to kill, Ashley did what she does best: packed some bags and decided to spend a few months in Colorado. By the time she was set to return to NYC, it was too late; Ashley had fallen in love with the blue skies and snow-capped peaks of Colorado—and had identified a pathway for herself into the cannabis industry.

Ashley began working as an independent consultant in the cannabis industry in 2014 when she co-developed two large scale cannabis events: CannaSearch, the largest cannabis career fair at the time, and The Marijuana for Medical Professionals Conference, a medical conference intended to educate healthcare professionals about cannabis efficacy and research. She went on to lead the Marketing, Retail and Operations teams for MiNDFUL—a large scale cultivator, extraction, and dispensary operator in Colorado.

While Ashley found her work at MiNDFUL to be incredibly fulfilling, in December of 2015 she made the decision to resume work as an independent consultant and founded Point Seven Group, a business solutions firm that works with operational and pre-license cannabis companies and teams around the country. The Point Seven team now supports clients throughout the country in the development of state application materials, license renewals, marketing and branding, web design, and cannabis business financial modeling.

Ashley specializes in operational efficiency and frequently trains and supports teams in reevaluating and reorganizing their cannabis entities to reduce costs and to optimize equipment and personnel. She enjoys developing and implementing standard operating procedures and training teams on sales and process efficiency. She is also developing the "Breaking the Grass Ceiling Speaker Series," which is set to launch at SXSW in Austin, Texas, in March 2017. The panel series will feature different women (some featured in this book) interested in sharing their stories with newcomers to the cannabis industry.

When not on the road working with clients, Ashley resides in Denver, Colorado, with her main squeeze, Alex, and their son—a french bulldog named Hamlet. She spends as much time as she can outdoors, climbing 14ers, backpacking, and running marathons for charity.

About the Author

LAUREN DEVINE IS a Massachusetts native, but, during her time as a professional actor, has traveled, worked, and lived in places all over the world, including New York City, Nashville, Connecticut, Toronto, and Shanghai. She holds a BFA in Musical Theatre from Syracuse University in upstate New York, where she graduated magna cum laude and with Renée Crown Honors. Lauren had a proclivity for drama and storytelling from an early age, impressing her parents' friends by performing bits of *Monty Python* scenes she rehearsed with her dad as well as writing poems and stories to give as gifts to her relatives. She published her first poem at eight years old: rhyming couplets about her exceptionally sharp memory entitled "My Magic Camera." Lauren has always enjoyed writing—winning several writing contests and awards in her youth—and continued her passion for the theatrical through college and adulthood. Lauren and her co-author, Ashley, grew up together in Massachusetts, but Lauren drifted to the stage while Ashley took to sports and student government. They came back together in the summer of 2016 to work as colleagues and to develop "Breaking the Grass Ceiling" as a platform for sharing stories and supporting women in their journey toward equality in the workplace.

For Lauren, the subject matter "Women, Weed & Business" was a thrilling combination of art, academia, and female empowerment. The stories of these women so inspired Lauren and her partner, Rollie, that the two have recently moved to Colorado to dive headfirst into the cannabis industry. Drawn by their mutual love and enthusiasm for marijuana and entrepreneurship, they continue to work alongside each other, building their own empire to share among their families and friends. They enjoy chillin' on the balcony; playing with their dog, Coco; cooking beautiful and delicious meals; and spending time "on Cape" at Miss B. Haven, Lauren's happy place in Harwichport, Cape Cod.

Acknowledgments

PHOTO CREDITS

Kristi Kelly - Anthony Camera Photography
Diane Czarkowski - Kim Sidwell of Cannabis Camera
Amy Dawn Bourlon-Hilterbran - Hand Photo: Mike Shatz; Family Photo: Nichole Montanez
Genifer Murray - Anthony Camera Photography
Amy Dilullo - Anthony Camera Photography
Betty Aldworth - Kim Sidwell of Cannabis Camera
Karin Lazarus - Povy Kendal Atchison
Heidi Keyes - Michael Reilly
Maureen McNamara - Andrea Flanagan
Ashley Picillo - Alex Witkowicz
Lauren Devine - Sean Turi

SPECIAL THANKS TO:

Emma Ritchie & Alex Witkowicz for their editorial support

Each contributor for her time, input and promotion

Blue Dream and Caffeine for their late night companionship and inspiration

Made in the USA
San Bernardino, CA
06 March 2017